Letters from

Pat Hennessy in his kitchen, CFC Lovat No. 2 Camp,
October 3, 1942 (Photo by Lieutenant Robert "Bob" Allen. Hennessy Moran Fonds, PANB)

■ Letters from Beauly

Pat Hennessy and the Canadian Forestry Corps in Scotland, 1940-1945

Melynda Jarratt

GOOSE LANE EDITIONS and
THE GREGG CENTRE FOR THE STUDY OF WAR AND SOCIETY

Edited by J. Brent Wilson.
Cover and page design by Chris Tompkins with Kerry Lawlor.

Front cover: Cooking crew, Indian Falls, Nepisiguit River, New Brunswick, 1930s: (left to right) Bert Wood, John Hanna, Pat Hennessy, Walter Glidden, and Peter Arseneault
Front and back cover: No. 15 Company, Canadian Forestry Corps. Scotland, August 1943. (Photo by the Service Photo Co, Pirbright, Surrey, 1815. Courtesy of Alfred Blizzard Jr.)

Photographs are provided courtesy of the Provincial Archives of New Brunswick (Hennessy Moran Fonds) except where noted. All photographs used by permission.

"G17024" by Fred Cogswell was published in *Systems of Value, Structures of Belief,* special issue of *Canadian Literature* 128 (Spring 1991). Reprinted by permission of Kathleen Forsythe.

Printed in Canada.
10 9 8 7 6 5 4 3 2 1

Library and Archives Canada Cataloguing in Publication
Jarratt, Melynda, author
    Letters from Beauly : Pat Hennessy and the Canadian Forestry Corps in Scotland, 1940-1945 / Melynda Jarratt.

Includes bibliographical references and index.
Issued in print and electronic formats.
Co-published by New Brunswick Military Heritage Project.
ISBN 978-0-86492-893-1 (paperback).--ISBN 978-0-86492-932-7 (epub).--ISBN 978-0-86492-933-4 (mobi)

    1. Hennessy, Pat, 1884-1970--Correspondence. 2. Canada. Canadian Army. Canadian Forestry Corps (1940-1945). 3. World War, 1939-1945--Personal narratives, Canadian. 4. World War, 1939-1945--War work--Scotland--Beauly. 5. World War, 1939-1945--War work--Canada. 6. Lumbermen--New Brunswick--Biography. 7. Farmers--New Brunswick--Biography. I. New Brunswick Military Heritage Project, issuing body II. Title. III. Title: Pat Hennessy and the Canadian Forestry Corps in Scotland, 1940-1945.

D768.153.J37 2016   940.54'1271   C2016-902444-X
                                                C2016-902445-8

The publishers and the author acknowledge the generous support of the Government of Canada, the Canada Council for the Arts, artsnb, and the Government of New Brunswick.

Goose Lane Editions
500 Beaverbrook Court, Suite 330
Fredericton, New Brunswick
CANADA E3B 5X4
www.gooselane.com

New Brunswick Military Heritage Project
The Brigadier Milton F. Gregg, VC,
Centre for the Study of War and Society
University of New Brunswick
PO Box 4400
Fredericton, New Brunswick
CANADA E3B 5A3
www.unb.ca/nbmhp

To my mother, Lucy (Hennessy) Jarratt of Bathurst, NB, and the late Fred Wilmot Hubbard of Burton, NB, born a month apart in 1917.

Their wartime memories of the people they loved helped me to write this book.

Contents

Introduction

*You Canadians may be cutting the Scots firs of the Highlands,
but in Highland hearts you are planting something far more
lasting.*

—Lady Laura Lovat, *Inverness Courier*, August 14, 1942

Letters from Beauly tells the story of Pat Hennessy's experiences during the Second World War and his nearly five years' service overseas as cook with 15 Company, Canadian Forestry Corps (CFC), on the northern Scottish estate of the famed Highland chief, Lord Lovat. It is not a military history of the CFC, nor is it an accounting of the CFC's logging operations in Scotland: as interesting as they might be, readers who want to pursue those parts of the CFC story should refer to William Wonders's excellent book, *Sawdust Fusiliers*, which is considered the seminal work on the subject.

The CFC is unique among the many specialized units that served in the two world wars. Made up primarily of English- and French-speaking loggers and foresters, they were experienced woodsmen who cut timber for the war effort in Scotland. During the Second World War, seven thousand men left the logging camps of rural Canada to serve in the CFC in Scotland. Nearly one thousand were from New Brunswick, and my grandfather, Patrick "Pat" Hennessy, was one of them.

This book began in summer 2008, when a chance search through the attic of our family's nineteenth-century homestead in Bathurst, New Brunswick, resulted in the discovery of nearly three hundred wartime letters written by and to my grandfather while he was serving in Scotland. An old man by comparison, Pat was fifty-six and the father of six adult children—three of whom would join the armed services themselves during the war—when he enlisted in the army in 1940. But in Pat's case, age didn't matter: he had more experience as a cook than anyone else, and that's what the army needed. He had worked every winter in the logging camps of northern New Brunswick since he was a youngster at the turn of the century, and every spring he'd run the drives, cooking meals in a makeshift boat that trailed behind the woodsmen along the river's edge. The CFC needed people like Pat, and despite his age, he was welcomed into the army. So began a five-year odyssey in Scotland that changed his life forever. There, Pat truly came into his own. For the first time, he was able to live the life he had always dreamed of, visiting Ireland, England, and Scotland, and establishing close friendships with the local people, especially the Frasers, with whom he developed a special bond.

As a family, we were astounded by the enormity of the collection in the attic. Not only did we find a treasure trove of personal letters, but the cache also included hundreds of archival photographs and documents—as well as a few boxes of heather! The entire collection was donated to the Provincial Archives of New Brunswick, and is called the Hennessy Moran Fonds in recognition of both my grandfather's and grandmother's sides of the family. And although the old homestead was turned over in 2010 to the Doucet Hennessy House Association—a charitable organization that aims to preserve and restore the heritage building—letters continue to be found in its nooks and crannies to this day, almost willing themselves to be read.

The letters are fascinating because they explore a heretofore unknown part of my grandfather's life in Beauly, Scotland, and the impact that he and thousands of other Canadian foresters had on Scotland—and vice versa—during the Second World War. As youngsters growing up in the baby boom era, we heard the stories of my grandfather's years in Scotland, of his meeting and attending church at Beaufort Castle at the invitation of Lady Lovat, wife of Lord Lovat, the British D-Day hero whom Churchill described as the "handsomest man who ever cut a throat." We always knew those years in Scotland were the best years of Pat's life, but we didn't know why. To see those experiences in writing, forty years after his death, was an affirmation of everything we knew to be true about the gentle man we called "Papa." It also explained to a great extent, how his wartime experiences shaped his postwar life in Canada, and those of his wife Beatrice and their children, for whom life would never be the same. The letters are a testament to the ties that bind people and families over time and space, through peace and war: how something once lost, when found, can change one's personal history and open doors to a world that can only be imagined, if one dares.

Pat Hennessy in his cook's uniform, outside
at a logging camp on the Little South Branch,
Nepisiguit River, NB, 1931

Chapter One

Pat Hennessy and 15 Company, Canadian Forestry Corps

Pat

Pat is our cook
And a good one at that
Can he put up the chuck
Well I'll say he can
He can make the pies
So they melt in your mouth
His stew is good
And so are his buns
His beans are first class
So here's to old Patty
The best of them all
May he carry on
For a good many falls
May he live three score more years and ten
And be happy and jolly every one of them

— Private H.A. Clewley, 15 Company, Canadian Forestry Corps

Patrick Hennessy was fifty-six years old and ready for a change when he joined the Canadian Forestry Corps (CFC) in December 1940. The Depression years hadn't been easy on "Pat," as he was known to his many friends and family in Bathurst, a town of thirty-five hundred people along the Bay of Chaleur in northeastern New Brunswick. The success of the two-hundred-acre mixed farm he and his wife Bea ran at the top of the St.

Peter's Village hill in West Bathurst depended on his steady employment with the Woodlands Division of the Bathurst Power and Paper Company (known to all as "the Company"). Somehow he'd managed to do it all for the nearly thirty years of their marriage, working as a cook in the logging camps of northern New Brunswick in the winter, on the logging runs in the spring, and on the tugboats between Bathurst and Gaspé, Quebec, in the summer.

Pat recalled the winter that a young Charlie Chamberlain — the well-known Canadian entertainer from Jacquet River — worked with him as a cookee. Charlie didn't last long in the camp, but he had a good sense of humour and — a sure way to Pat's heart — knew all the old Irish ballads, so he could entertain for hours at a time while peeling potatoes. Charlie and Pat remained friends for life.

But there was no work for anyone the winter of 1937-38. The Depression had hit the forestry industry particularly hard in New Brunswick, so Pat went to Saint John, where his wife's brother, John Moran, found him employment as a roofer in the shipyards. It was an outside job in the wind and cold, and it must have been tough for a man who had spent most of his working life by the heat of a big camp stove. Back in Bathurst, the large mixed farm, with its abundant apple orchards, vegetable gardens, and berries, kept the family fed. There was income from the sale of produce as well as hay, oats, buckwheat, and bales of straw. They sold calves and piglets, ducks, geese, chickens and eggs, cream and butter. They even ran a milk route twice a day — during the worst years of the Depression, they gave away milk to locals whose suffering was palpable. Pat and the other men in the family also dug graves for recently departed Catholics in the parish: it paid well at $2 each (about $30 today), but it was sporadic work, and extremely difficult in the winter when the frozen ground had to be softened with bonfires — sometimes even dynamite. With few alternatives, Pat stayed in Saint John that winter, thankful for a steady paycheque, which he faithfully sent to his wife back in Bathurst.

Pat had a grade three education, having left the one-room schoolhouse to work as a cookee in the Miramichi logging camps at the turn of the century. He was a woodsman, a farmer, a loving father to his children, and devout Roman Catholic who loved to sing and play the piano. He counted among his friends Monsignor William Varrily, as well as the many parish priests and nuns of Holy Family Church located across the street from the Hennessy family homestead.

Pat was born in Keenan, Northumberland County, in 1884, one of seven children of William and Mary Anne (Vickers) Hennessy, fourth-generation Irish-Canadians. Pat's parents were farmers and shoemakers, as were his Hennessy grandparents and great-grandparents, who had made their way to Bonaventure, Quebec, from Ireland sometime in the late 1700s. William, Pat's grandfather, came to the Miramichi in the 1830s and married Pat's Scottish ancestor, Elizabeth Urquhart, whose childhood story of being orphaned at sea and then adopted by David and Helen (Hierlihy) Savoie of Tabusintac, New Brunswick, in 1818 was the stuff of family legend. After Pat married Beatrice "Bea" Moran in August 1911, they bought the large, two-hundred-acre farm and homestead in Bathurst in partnership with Bea's uncle, Manus Kane of South Tetagouche.

Every winter Pat left home to work in the lumber camps upriver, and every spring he cooked on a floating raft that trailed the river runs until planting began. In the summer, he was the cook on tugboats with names like the *Cascapedia*, the *Nippy*, and the *Peggy L*, which hauled log booms from Gaspé to the sawmill in Bathurst. When harvest season came, he worked the farm, preparing for winter, until it was time to return to the woods.

In September 1939, Pat and Bea had six living children. The eldest, Roger, age twenty-four, worked at Bathurst Power and Paper as a draftsman. But what Roger really wanted to be was an artist. As a child, he had always dabbled in art, but it was at the private, French-language Collège Sacré-Coeur in Bathurst where his talents were put to good use creating a lavishly decorated book reminiscent of the insular art produced by Irish monks in the illuminated Book of Kells. A prolific artist who was comfortable in traditional and commercial art forms, Roger Hennessy's portraits and landscapes are in private collections throughout Canada and the United States.

Lucy, then twenty-two, had graduated from the private Sacred Heart Academy in Bathurst in 1936, at the height of the Depression and, armed

The Hennessy family: (from left to right) Roger Hennessy, James Moran,
Lucy Hennessy, Pat Hennessy (holding Anna), young Manus Hennessy,
Anna Moran, Manus Kane, and Beatrice (Moran) Hennessy;
Pabineau Falls, NB, circa 1920

with a commercial certificate, she found full-time employment as a medical
secretary for Dr. Lambert "Bert" Densmore, past president of the Canadian
Medical Council. The well-known doctor and veteran of the First World
War had been awarded the Military Cross for his service with the Medical
Corps in France, and elected the first president of the Bathurst Legion
when it formed in 1927.

Anna, age twenty, had also graduated from the commercial program
at Sacred Heart Academy, and was working for the Bathurst Power and
Paper Company's Woodlands Division at the foot of St. Peter's Village
hill, where she was secretary to the woods manager, L.A. Nix. During
the war years, Mr. Nix sent care packages every Christmas to the dozens
of Company men who had joined the services. Anna was responsible for
preparing the gift boxes, filling them to the brim with canned lobster,

Ganong chocolates, and other New Brunswick delights. She also composed the letters, including those to her own father, which began "Dear Pat."

Seventeen-year-old James, known as "Bunny," was just beginning his last year of high school at the Free School when war was declared. Bunny was the first of the Hennessy children to attend public school, a result of the tighter economic circumstances in the midst of the Depression. Fourteen-year-old Bruno, independent minded and rebellious, had quit school in grade seven and was begrudgingly helping out on the farm. But Bobby, almost ten years old, was still at Holy Family School, the Catholic school across the street from the Hennessy homestead. Three other children had died: the first born, Manus, named after his great-uncle Manus Kane, passed away from tuberculosis on Good Friday 1932, just a few months short of his twentieth birthday. Two-year-old Varrily, named after Monsignor Varrily, injured his head in a fall and died before Christmas 1929; and Dorothy died of pneumonia in 1922 when she was just ten months old.

Bea's eight-year-old nephew, Tommy Moran, was also living with the Hennessys in Bathurst. Tommy's father was killed in 1938 in an industrial accident at Atlantic Sugar, and the family was split up, one child staying with his mother Margaret in Saint John while Tommy was sent to live with Bea and Pat during the war years.

The harsh reality of farming life probably wasn't what Bea expected when she married Pat Hennessy. Like her husband, Bea was fourth-generation Irish, with roots in County Kildare. She also had a Scottish ancestor: her great-grandfather, Alexander Fraser, who was born in 1799 and emigrated to Canada as a young man. But that is where their similarities ended: Bea was from Blissfield, a tiny Irish settlement along the Miramichi River between Blackville and Doaktown. There, her father was a well-educated gentleman farmer and postmaster who built a one-room schoolhouse so his four sons and three daughters could get an education close to home. A licensed teacher, Bea graduated from the Normal School in Fredericton in 1909, and went on to teach at a one-room schoolhouse in South Tetagouche, another Irish settlement near Bathurst, where she lived with her uncle, Alexander "Alec" Kane, and her aunt Nora Kane.

Bea and Pat met at a dance in Blackville, where young people from surrounding Irish settlements would gather to celebrate New Year's and St. Patrick's Day. They corresponded by "postals"—postcards that were becoming increasingly popular at the time. Their first child, Manus, was born in Tetagouche in 1912. By 1914, Bea and Pat had the big house and farm in Bathurst with Bea's Uncle Manus, a bachelor who had worked in California and returned to Canada determined to establish a successful farm with his young niece and her husband.

Bea, too, had big dreams: she established a fancy millinery shop in a separate building on the property that at one time had been operated as a grocery store by its former owners, Francis and Marie (Haché) McManus. Mr. McManus was a university-educated teacher-turned-politician who represented Gloucester County as Liberal member of Parliament in the second and third legislatures following Confederation. Situated across the street from Holy Family Church, on the highest point of land at the juncture of what is now St. Peter Avenue and St. Anne Street, the property was on a prominent commercial spot and an excellent location to set up business. Bea ran the millinery shop in the converted grocery store, putting advertisements in the local *Northern Light* newspaper for "Fine Millinery." A photograph taken about 1919 shows a group of finely dressed men and women with a hand painted sign, "Mrs. P.J. Hennessy Millinery" in the background. Pat was gone most of the year, however, so the long days and hard work demanded by both the farm and her young family forced Bea to give up her dream and settle for the life of a farmer's wife. She couldn't have predicted the loneliness of married life, or the personal tragedies that would befall her young family over the following years. Her husband's long absences surely made running the farm difficult, but to bear the loss of three children on her own would have been heartbreaking.

When Bea's Uncle Manus—her benefactor, co-worker, and co-owner of the homestead—also died of tuberculosis in March 1933, Bea was the only grown-up left in the family. In the absence of an adult male, she became sole decision-maker and head of the household, managing the finances, maintenance, and repairs of the large house and barns, running the farm with its fields and animals, hiring and firing labourers, and guiding her children's education by tutoring them after school. The private school educations of Roger, Lucy, and Anna also had to be paid for, and Pat's monthly income of $100 was an integral part of the fiscal balancing act without which the whole operation would have collapsed.

After the cold winter of 1937-38 in Saint John, word came that the Company was hiring again for the winter of 1938-39. Pat jumped at the opportunity to get back to what he knew best: cooking in the logging camps of northern New Brunswick.

Nineteen thirty-nine also marked the beginning of the Second World War, and as experienced woodsmen started to enlist after Canada declared war in September, their absence became increasingly evident in the lumbering industry. Things weren't the same in the woods the winter and spring of 1939-40, and Pat wasn't happy about it at all. As the loggers he had worked with for years joined the army, the men were replaced by inexperienced, younger crew who griped about everything, including the food. Pat had worked in the woods since he was twelve years old, and his cooking had never been questioned before. The old friends were gone, replaced by a new, fickle generation that Pat said "had some nerve to complain when they had all just survived a Depression." So, when the winter logging was over and the spring run finished for another year, Pat was left wondering what he was going to do after the summer tugboat season ended.

He didn't have long to wonder: in July 1940 articles appeared in New Brunswick papers announcing the creation of a Forestry Corps for service overseas in Scotland. The local Bathurst magistrate, Major G.H. Willett, a First World War veteran of the 165th Battalion (Acadiens), Canadian Expeditionary Force, had received a commission to mobilize a two-hundred-man battalion of the Canadian Forestry Corps in spring 1940. After the announcement about the CFC appeared in the newspapers, a large number of local men made arrangements to join the unit under Major Willett's command. But to everyone's disappointment, in mid-July the major was discharged as medically unfit. Still, that didn't seem to stop him from assisting with recruitment at the armoury on Main Street, just a short walk down the hill and across the bridge from the Hennessy homestead.

For a man whose travels had been limited to one trip to Montreal and his honeymoon in Boston thirty years before, Scotland must have seemed a far-off place, but Pat made up his mind to join, and he was eager to go. It was the Old Country, after all, and it was close to Ireland, where his own people were from; besides, Bea had roots in Scotland. He might not find his Urquhart roots, but surely he would find her Fraser relatives in the Highlands.

The newspaper articles said, however, that recruits had to be age forty-five or under, in good health, and have logging experience. Pat was more than qualified, but even though he was strong and healthy, with a full head of black hair, he was eleven years past the age limit. But the CFC proved not to be so strict about the age requirements. After a word of advice from Major Willett, and perhaps a telephone call to higher authorities, Pat suddenly lost seven years from his age. As his attestation papers show, Pat claimed to be born on January 8, 1891, thus becoming a more acceptable age of forty-nine – a lie that would come back to haunt Pat when he applied for old age pension at age sixty-five.

That summer and fall of 1940, as Pat prepared the farm for winter and waited for the call to go to basic training at Valcartier, Quebec, family dynamics were already starting to shift, signalling the beginning of change that would transform the Hennessys and their farm during the war. In July, Roger, then twenty-five, married Eileen O'Toole of Bathurst, and before long enlisted in the Air Force. Lucy became engaged to her long-time beau, Sidney Jarratt, and in August, Anna met a Norwegian merchant mariner, Henrik Wesenberg, igniting a romance that endured the war years. That September, Bunny was eighteen, and the challenge would be to keep him on the farm while all of his friends joined up. Then there was Bruno, who at sixteen was starting to get into trouble, hanging around with a bad crowd and staying out late at night. Bobby, the youngest at eleven, was no stranger to hard work, and would often shoulder the burden of farm labour over the next few years. But he didn't want to be a farmer: Bobby was going to be a doctor.

Michael   Patrick   Mary   Jack   George
                     Ann

The Hennessy brothers, Michael, Pat, Jack, and George, with their mother, Mary Ann (Vickers) Hennessy, at the family homestead on the Howard Road, Blackville, NB, September 1940

On December 8, 1940, the day Pat left for Fredericton to join the Forestry Corps, his ninety-year-old mother, Mary Ann (Vickers) Hennessy, passed away at his brother George's home, on the Howard Road near Blackville. Although Pat had already made a visit to the Miramichi to say his goodbyes, nothing could have prepared him for the shock of losing his mother on the eve of his departure. Was it an omen of things to come? As it came time to leave for the train that would take him to Military District 7 (MD7) Depot in Fredericton, the first leg of his journey to Scotland, Pat was overcome by emotion. Bobby recalled his father holding him tightly and sobbing. A pall of sadness fell over the family: their father was leaving for a war overseas, their grandmother Hennessy had just died, and Pat couldn't even attend the funeral. He had to leave for Valcartier. There was no going back.

That same day Pat wrote the first of what would become a massive collection of letters by and to him from family members and friends over the course of the Second World War. In this first letter, we see the beginning of a pattern that was to repeat itself time and again over the next five years. Despite his poor spelling and changing wartime circumstances, Pat's letters never strayed too far from major themes: news about his work and surroundings, comments about the children, concern for the family farm, the progress of the war, and love to all.

December 8, 1940
Dear Bee

Arrived safe. The train was six hours late. We were one hour late. We were supposed to be at the Barracks at 6 o'clock but it was seven when we reported. All the bunch was along so they did not say anything to us.

Well Bee we had a tiresome trip up. The train was so crowded. Eileen was up to the train. Roger was not feeling well she said.

I suppose the boys have gone back to school again.

Oh yes you can tell Bruno to let the cow loose in the barn.

How are the girls? Has James gone up yet? Today is fine and cool. I am going to work tonight. Nearly all the men are back again. The *Maritime* had 20 coaches on and all loaded coming up last night.

Well Bee this is all for now I will find out tomorrow about the Rosary Hall. I will go out to town tomorrow. Good bye. Love to all.

Pat

At Fredericton, Pat officially became part of the army by signing his attestation papers at MD7. From there he was sent to Valcartier, Quebec, arriving on December 12. Only four days had passed since his departure from Bathurst and the terrible news of his mother's death, but Pat was ready to put it behind him. Finding friends from Bathurst and down shore at Camp Valcartier, as well as officers who treated him with kindness and respect, made it easier to adjust. On his first day of work, he was looking forward to the future and a completely different life as a cook in the Canadian Army.

December 13, 1940

Dear Bee

Arrived last night at 5:30 o'clock. The train was 4 hours late. I traveled with a Mr. Samson from Fredericton. Well there is a lot of men here I know from down shore and Eddie O'Toole is here. I saw them all last night. Major Williams is a fine man. He is just what Major Willett said of him. Well I like it here. I go to work at 7 o'clock tonight. I start as night cook for a few nights. Well I got on good at Fredericton. I just stayed one night. Every one seems so nice. All the officers are so nice.

How are the boys making out? How are the girls? How did they make out when you was away? I will write again. I have to go to work soon.

Bye Bye

How is Bobby and Bruno and Tom? Tell them to be good boys.

Yours PJH

That first Christmas at Valcartier was no different for Pat than any other Christmas over the past thirty years of his married life. Working in the logging camps during the winter was a commitment that included Christmas and New Year's Day, so it was a rare occasion that Pat was home for the holidays with his wife and children. He didn't come home the Christmas of 1929, when two-year-old Varrily died, nor did he make it home for the funeral of his oldest and much loved son Manus at Easter 1932. Only once, in 1935, at the request of his five-year-old son Bobby, did Pat get to enjoy the semblance of Christmas at home with family; that was the year the tree stayed up until April, closed off in the parlour—the coldest room of the house—with all the decorations and Pat's unwrapped presents underneath.

This year, like all the Christmases gone by and the ones to come during the war years ahead, Pat served dinner to a group of men on Christmas Eve. Only the numbers were different: this time, six hundred. Major C.A. "Archie" Williams had gone home for the holidays. But "Bob Allen," as Pat called the young second lieutenant, Robert Kenneth Allen—his son Roger's friend and co-worker from the Woodlands Division in Bathurst, who would become a good friend of Pat's in Scotland—was there, and so too were a lot of the boys Pat knew from Bathurst and down shore. The army was his family now.

Chapter Two

From Valcartier to Scotland

One tree is required to provide a soldier with living quarters, a mess room and a recreation hall. A second is needed to make wooden crates to ship his food, clothing and his share of tanks, guns and ammunition. Three trees are converted into high explosives, gunstocks, wood for training planes, building ships, factories and so forth which help him in the fighting line, directly or indirectly.

—*Aberdeen Press and Journal*, November 23, 1944

The Canadian Forestry Corps was Britain's answer to a wartime crisis in the availability of wood products, brought on by the German occupation of the Baltic. One of the world's largest importers of wood products, Britain had come to rely on Russia, Finland, Estonia, Latvia, and Lithuania for its peacetime requirements. Of immediate concern was the supply of pit props for the coal-mining industry, without which the entire country would grind to a halt. With Germany in control of Baltic waters, and the additional wartime demand outstripping Britain's ability to supply its own needs, the wood had to be replaced somehow. But in the midst of the deadly Battle of the Atlantic, every ship was at a premium, and bringing in lumber from Canada was not a viable option. The solution was found in the massive forest plantations of Scotland's Highland estates.

Further complicating matters, experienced loggers and professional foresters in Britain had rushed to enlist at the declaration of war in September 1939, leaving a skills gap that had to be met. Newfoundland was the first to answer the call for help, with 2,150 men of the Newfoundland Forestry Unit in service by summer 1940. Other countries with a tradition of forestry operations also sent lumbermen, including New Zealand, Australia, Norway, and

Canadian Forestry Corps, Second World War

Unit No (Coy.)	Canadian Mobilization Point	Mobilization Date	Arrived in Scotland	Ceased Operations in Scotland	Camps Occupied in Scotland (relocation dates indicated)
1**	Ottawa, ON	16 Jul 1940	28 Feb 1941	14 Jun 1944	Cawdor North (Dallaschyle), Croy; Skibo B, Spinningdale (28 Oct 1943)
2*	Westmount, QC	Jul 1940	1 Mar 1941	1 Oct 1943	Ballogie No 2, Aboyne
3*	Quebec City, QC	12 Jul 1940	20 Apr 1941	30 Sep 1943	Ballogie No 1, Aboyne
4	Newcastle, NB	15 Jul 1940	20 Apr 1941	20 Mar 1945	Glentanar, Dinnet; Cooperhill, Forres (21 Nov 1944)
5**	Port Arthur, ON	10 Jul 1940	26 Dec 1940	1 Apr 1944	Black Island, Blair Atholl; Insh, Kincraig (16 Dec 1943)
6	Victoria, BC	12 Jul 1940	1 Mar 1941	25 May 1945	Bog of Shannon, Avoch; Abernethy, Boat of Garten (10 Jul 1943)
7*	Victoria, BC	14 Aug 1940	1 Mar 1941	7 Oct 1943	Highwood (Feabuie), Culloden
8*	Ottawa, ON	17 Jul 1940	1 Mar 1941	7 Oct 1943	Cawdor South (Inchyettle), Cawdor
9**	Westmount, QC	2 Aug 1940	20 Apr 1941	9 Jun 1944	Lamington Park, Tain; Berriedale (27 Jan 1943); Lamington Park, Tain (24 Nov 1943)
10	Vancouver, BC	1 Aug 1940	2 Jul 1941	16 Jun 1945	Dochfour, Inverness
11	Haileybury, ON	10 Aug 1940	20 Apr 1941	26 May 1945	Dall, Kinloch Rannoch; Carrbridge (11 Dec 1942)
12*	Kirkland Lake, ON	12 Aug 1940	2 Jul 1941	1 Oct 1943	Insh, Kincraig
13	Halifax, NS	13 Aug 1940	2 Jul 1941	17 Mar 1945	Southesk, Brechin; Orrin Bridge, Muir of Ord (8 Nov 1943); Skibo B, Spinningdale (15 Jul 1944); Orrin Bridge, Muir of Ord (14 Nov 1944)
14**	Sudbury, ON	20 Aug 1940	2 Jul 1941	22 Jun 1944	Wilderness (Balnagown), Milton; Abernethy, Boat of Garten (19 Nov 1942)
15**	Chatham, NB	20 Aug 1940	20 Apr 1941	1 Apr 1944	Lovat No 2 (Boblainy), Kiltarlity
16**	Quebec City, QC	16 Aug 1940	2 Jul 1941	1 Apr 1944	Blackhall, Banchory
17*	Fort Frances, ON	18 Aug 1940	20 Apr 1941	30 Sep 1943	Rosehall, Invershin
18	Victoria, BC	Aug 1940	20 Apr 1941	26 May 1945	Lovat No 1 (Teanacoil), Kiltarlity
19	Edmonton, AB	6 Sept 1940	2 Jul 1941	21 Apr 1945	Belladrum, Kiltarlity
20	Saskatoon, SK	2 Oct 1940	2 Jul 1941	21 Mar 1945	Torwood, Kincraig; Nethybridge (12 Jun 1942)
21*		7 Nov 1941	27 Dec 1941	2 Oct 1943	Orrin Bridge, Muir of Ord
22		7 Jan 1942	20 Jan 1942	28 May 1945	Abergeldie (Balmoral), Ballater; Blackhall, Banchory (14 Jun 1944); Abernethy, Boat of Garten (30 Nov 1944)
23*		Jan 1942	20 Jan 1942	2 Oct 1943	Darnaway, Forres
24		Mar 1942	30 Mar 1942	21 Apr 1945	Abergeldie (Balmoral), Ballater; Lovat No 2 (Boblainy), Kiltarlity (15 Jun 1944)
25**	Fredericton, NB	16 Mar 1942	30 Mar 1942	14 Jun 1944	Mar Lodge, Braemar
26*		Jun 1942	25 Jun 1942	1 Oct 1943	Skibo C, Clashmore
27**		30 Jun 1942	9 Oct 1942	13 Jun 1944	Cooperhill, Forres
28**		16 May 1942	26 May 1942	1 Apr 1944	Ardersier, Nairn
29**		May 1942	26 May 1942	29 Sept 1943	Skibo B, Spinningdale
30**		May 1942	11 Jun 1942	1 Apr 1944	Skibo A, Spinningdale

* - returned to Canada, October 1943
** - continued operations in North-West Europe
Sources: CFC War Diaries (LAC RG 24, Vol. 16,419-16,450).

The thirty companies of the Canadian Forestry Corps were recruited from every province in the Dominion. Three were mobilized in New Brunswick: 4 Company in Newcastle, 15 Company in Chatham, and 25 Company in Fredericton. (William Wonders, *Sawdust Fusiliers*) even British Honduras. An additional five thousand female recruits, called "Lumber Jills," were trained as part of the Women's Land Army Timber Corps to work the forests of Britain. But the largest number of professional loggers and foresters came from Canada, the majority arriving in 1941.

Almost seven thousand lumbermen from across the Dominion joined the Canadian Forestry Corps during the Second World War. Nearly 14 percent were from New Brunswick, a disproportionate contribution for a province with a population of fewer than five hundred thousand. From British Columbia to Cape Breton, the lumbermen were following the example set in the First World War, when nearly thirty-five thousand Canadians served overseas with the CFC in Britain and on the continent.

Starting in July 1940, twenty companies consisting of two hundred men each were formed. Two of the companies were from New Brunswick: 4 Company, based at Newcastle, and 15 Company in Chatham. Between November 1941 and May 1942, another ten companies were raised, including 25 Company in Fredericton. The first to arrive in Scotland was an advance party in October 1940, followed by 5 Company in late December, setting the stage for the full compliment of thirty companies that made their way to Scotland during the war years. No matter where they came from or how old they were, every CFC recruit received basic training at Camp Valcartier, where they were either turned into soldiers or sent back home. Located about twenty-five kilometres outside Quebec City, Valcartier was well known to the generation of the First World War as the primary training base for the First Canadian Contingent in 1914. During the Second World War, it became the Canadian Infantry Training Centre and the place where Forestry Corps recruits went to undergo basic training before leaving for Scotland.

Due to a shortage of space at Valcartier, when Pat and troops from several other CFC companies arrived on December 12, 1940, they were stationed at the immigration building at Louise Basin, near Quebec City. It was another two months before 15 Company moved to Valcartier, but not before five more Forestry Corps companies (1, 2, 6, 7, and 8) departed for Scotland on February 6, 1941. In William Wonders's seminal book on the history of the Canadian Forestry Corps, *The Sawdust Fusiliers*, P.H. Morely, former lieutenant and training officer with 11 Company recalls that the companies billeted in the immigration building were "greatly envied by others because we were 'living in civilization.' Whatever the case the presumed envy was certainly not because of our living quarters. The immigration building had been condemned after the First World War and was probably a real fire trap." Pat didn't like the immigration building, or "shed," as he called it, either. Within ten days of his arrival, he was complaining about the billet, saying it couldn't get "more cold." "There is a lot sick here with the cold. We have a poor barracks here. It is a concrete building, just like sleeping in a green cellar, damp and cold no ventilation at all." By the third week of January, Pat wrote home to Bea that the troops were "corteened" (quarantined) for twenty days due to an outbreak of chicken pox and all leave to Quebec City was cancelled. This interfered with Bea's explicit instructions to find an Eaton's store in Quebec City where Pat was expected to make some purchases of material that couldn't be found back home in Bathurst.

On February 7, the quarantine was lifted, and an advance party, consisting of about fifty to sixty troops, including Pat, was advised to prepare for a move the next day to Sussex, New Brunswick. Pat wrote to Bea, telling her he would write when he got settled in, but it never happened. On the morning of the eighth, in a hastily written letter, Pat wrote to say that the advance party had been cancelled because they were all quarantined again due to a case of spinal "meginis": "You know what it is. I can't spell it."

After three weeks in quarantine, the troops were getting restless. No sooner was the prohibition lifted than trouble erupted on the streets of Quebec City. Pat saved a newspaper article from February 6, 1941, that described a fist fight that broke out in a Quebec City restaurant between two members of the Highland Light Infantry (HLI) from Brantford, Ontario, that left one man injured. According to Lieutenant-Colonel G.F. Berteau, assistant adjutant and quartermaster-general of Military District 5, two soldiers of the HLI got into a fight in a rue Saint-Jean café after one threw a glass of beer into the other's face. The disturbance spilled out onto the street and a crowd gathered. The municipal police arrested the two soldiers, and some force had to be used to place them in confinement. Later, these soldiers were released and disciplined by their commanding officer. In an attempt to quell concerns that the fight was language related, Major G.O. Bigaouette, director of police for the Quebec military district, was reported as saying "the fracas was entirely between English-speaking soldiers." But with so many English-speaking troops in the heart of French-speaking Canada, conflicts were inevitable.

Two days later, about fifteen members of the same Highland unit sought their revenge on Quebec City municipal police officers for the arrest "by force" of their comrades. The Highlanders returned to the same rue Saint-Jean café where their friends had been arrested, "and having bolstered themselves with a few drinks, decided to look for the police." The group of fifteen soon grew to five hundred, and turned into an hour-long, all-out street battle between Highlanders and police that included the use of tear-gas bombs at the height of the disorder. Realizing he and his men were outnumbered, Major Bigaouette, who himself had been injured in the disturbance, called for reinforcements from two companies of the Canadian Forestry Corps stationed nearby. Two officers, one from 11 Company and another from 15 Company, Captain Clair M. Young of South Devon, New Brunswick, were quickly dispatched with some Forestry Corps men to quell the disturbance, but by the time they arrived, order had been restored. To prevent any further occurrences, military piquets made up of CFC troops and others were set up around the city that week to "reassure the civilian population that the Military Authorities are able to look after any of their own troubles." As the 15 Company diarist observed, "there were more soldiers in the piquets than there were on the streets."

15 Company wasn't without its own problems. That month, more than a dozen men were punished, mostly for being absent without leave, but others under the more serious violation of "conduct to the prejudice of good order and military discipline." One man, who created a disturbance by fighting with other soldiers, was given twenty-eight days' detention and had to forfeit twenty-eight days' pay, a huge sum in those days.

Although the immigration shed at Quebec City had its drawbacks, its location so close to the city and all its amenities made it preferable to Valcartier—at least for the men. The officers, however, had their misgivings about the change of venue: "It is with divided opinion that

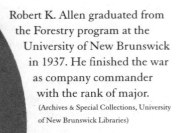

Robert K. Allen graduated from the Forestry program at the University of New Brunswick in 1937. He finished the war as company commander with the rank of major.
(Archives & Special Collections, University of New Brunswick Libraries)

we consider the move," wrote the 15 Company war diarist. "We have been comfortable and our stay in Quebec City generally pleasant. What camp life will be, few of us know." On February 15 Pat wrote "we got orders last night" that the company was leaving on the seventeenth for Valcartier. Pat went with the advance party headed by Lieutenant Allen, Roger's friend from Bathurst Power and Paper, whom Pat was getting to know very well.

Robert Kenneth "Bob" Allen graduated from the University of New Brunswick's Forestry School in 1937. It was a bad time for a young man to be looking for a job in the forest industry, but he managed to find work with the Woodlands Division of Bathurst Power and Paper, cruising the woods for timber. In August 1940, Allen enlisted with 15 Company at Chatham, was commissioned as a lieutenant, and became the forest engineer for the unit. From Chatham, Allen and the rest of the company were transferred to Quebec City; when Pat arrived that December, they had already been in the immigration building for nearly three months. Another two months passed before 15 Company moved to Valcartier; by February 20, the main body of 11, 12, 13, and 15 Companies was settled at Valcartier in the "A" area. The officers didn't like it, but Pat, accustomed to a rough life in the logging camps, was pleased as could be: "[W]e been here a few day now

Pat Hennessy (left) and another cook in front of Hut #404,
Camp Valcartier, Quebec, winter 1941

we like it fine. It is 25 miles out of town in the country. Well Bee we are all well. The days here are awful fine. Just like April. The snow is melting fast. I don't imagine we will be here long now. We will be moving somewhere for the officers don't like it here. I like it better here than in the city. The place is cleaner and the air is better."

The food wasn't bad either. The menu for February 24-March 2 consisted of hearty fare that Pat would have been familiar with in the logging camps; every day began with a breakfast of rolled oats, bacon and eggs and fried potatoes, bread and jam, and coffee. For variety, there were prunes, corn syrup, scrambled eggs, toast, and honey; dinner and supper were fit for a king, with roast beef, pork, fish, stew, dessert, and tea on the menu. A light meal finished off the day.

Pat was right at home in his new military surroundings. In a letter to his daughter Lucy, Pat described the camp, which reminded him of the Company houses in Bathurst: "This place here is like a little town, all

Pat's son Roger drew this certificate for 15 Company in 1941. It was a big hit with the officers, who paid $5 apiece for their own copy.

Bobby, Pat, and Lucy, outside the Hennessy homestead, March 1940, on Pat's last trip to Bathurst before leaving for Scotland. A CFC cap badge is clearly visible.

huts. Each hut holds about 150 men and one cook house feeds 400 men. We have 15 and 13 company. 13 is from Nova Scotia. The huts are all numbered. Ours is 423, 424, 425. The huts are all alike in rows and streets something like the bungalows at the pulp mill."

Pat had other reasons to be happy: in February he passed his trades test, and was reclassified as Cook "C," which meant an increase in pay. He was also getting along very well with the enlisted men and officers, with whom he had developed a friendly relationship. Pat's son, Roger, the artist, created an original watercolour certificate for 15 Company with a woodpecker on a tree stump in the forest. The certificate could be customized with room for a photograph and the person's name. The drawings were a huge success among the officers, and the demand was so great that Pat wrote back to Bea twice in February with requests for Roger to make more: "They were all crazy about it," Pat said, "Two of the officers wants one."

In mid-March, rumours made their way around camp that all leaves were to be cancelled and that 15 Company was moving to Debert, Nova Scotia, en route to Halifax and then overseas. Pat had expected nine days' furlough at the end of the month, so he wrote Lucy to say that, no matter what happened, he would let her know when the train was expected to pass through Bathurst, so the family could meet him at the train station. This would be Pat's last chance to see everyone before going overseas, and it meant a lot to him to say his final goodbyes in person. The rumours turned out to be false, however, and Pat got his furlough at the end of March, his first time home since December.

Pat returned to Valcartier on March 28, and was no sooner back in camp when 15 Company got the word, for real this time, to move, only straight from Valcartier to Halifax, with no stopover at Debert. As the train wound its way into the Bathurst train station, Pat found his youngest daughter Anna in the crowd alongside the track. He stayed just long enough to give Anna his wedding ring for safekeeping. Bea, Roger, and Eileen were there, too, but in the confusion Pat didn't see any of them.

Upon arrival at Halifax later that morning, 15 Company immediately boarded the MS *Batory*, a Polish passenger ship of the Gdynia-America line that would take the men on the next leg of their journey overseas. Originally designed to carry seven hundred passengers, the *Batory* had been converted into an Allied troopship, and would carry four thousand servicemen on this sailing. On April 7, Pat wrote to Bea from the ship, saying they were expecting to leave any moment and asking her to "Pray for me." Early in the morning of April 10, the *Batory* slipped out of Halifax Harbour and joined a convoy headed out into the North Atlantic. Alongside was the powerful battleship, HMS *Rodney*, a stark reminder of the jeopardy that awaited everyone in the darkest days of the Battle of the Atlantic.

Fortunately, the journey was without incident, and there were no signs of enemy raiders, either by sea or by air. On board, Pat had a stateroom complete with bathroom, shower, and four beds. He also met a few familiar faces, including his young nephews Hubert and Elbridge Hennessy of Campbellton, and a friend from Doaktown, Major Ralph Holmes of 17 Company. Holmes had been recruited out of Fort Frances, Ontario, where he had moved in the 1920s to work in the lumbering industry there. When Ralph needed more men for 17 Company, he found them in the Miramichi, so the unit was a mix of Ontario and New Brunswick men. Pat was notorious for getting seasick on the Company tugboats between Bathurst and Quebec, but to his surprise he fared well on the ocean crossing. In a letter to daughter Anna, Pat wanted everyone to know it, especially Percy Adams, the engineer on the *Nippy*: "I was sea sick," he wrote, "but I got over it. Tell Percy I'm a sailor now."

In his first long letter to Bea, written from the Scottish Highlands more than a month after arrival, Pat describes his journey across the Atlantic.

We saw lots of whales and sharks. The sea gulls followed us all the way across. Oh, the Atlantic Ocean is marvelous to see just at that time of the year. Wasn't it rough by times. One would almost roll out of bed and every time she would roll over on her side. You could hear the next fellow getting sick. We passed Newfoundland at night. I do not know if one could see it or not. Ah, what a stretch of water for days and days nothing but the blue sea. Nothing in sight but the convoy and whales blowing and sea gulls flying around. Elbridge Hennessy was on the boat 2 days before I knew he was on. He got lost on the boat and was looking for his room. He come down on the deck when I was passed by and on his way back I knew him and he did me at the same time. Wasn't he glad to see me. We were together all the way across. Major Holmes came with us too. He is somewhere in Scotland.

He goes on to describe the beauty of the flora and fauna in Scotland and nearby bombing raids, and mentions news of Rudolf Hess, the German deputy führer who, to everyone's surprise, landed his Messerschmitt Bf 110 fighter near Glasgow on May 10, 1941, in an ill-fated one-man mission to negotiate peace with the British.

Ah, yes, the Clyde River is just too grand for words. Its green banks, its high towering light houses and the beautiful little villages all along both sides. Greenock is a lovely place, a nice town. Then we took a train. Ah, the lovely country side. Glasgow on the Clyde, is it ever nice and Ayr where Bobby Burns was born! The house is there yet, it is a park now. Glasgow is where Hess landed, it is about 100 miles from here. I suppose you know more about it then we do. Jerry was over us last night but he did not lay an egg. I guess he did a few miles away. I suppose you heard it on the radio before this will get to you. Well the country is beautiful...it is all farms with great flocks of sheep. Some lovely sheep dogs to herd them....The stone fences and hedges run for miles through the country and they have been built for years. They call them dykes. There are just a few small birds, black birds, robins, swamp robins, a few others I don't know their names, but awful beautiful. There are lots of wild pigeons. They are two times as big as tame ones. There are wild turkeys, awful wild, also pheasants and partridges. Bee I wish you could be here to see. It is so much nicer than one can imagine. The trees are black birch, jack pine, lime, oak, beech, juniper. They call them larch. Oh, but the holly tree is nice and green. There are some berries on from last year yet. The heather is starting to bloom good now.

He also talks about the people he is starting to meet, and ends with a plea for mittens, certain he's going to need them in the cold winter that is sure to come.

Yes, for the people are awful nice to us here. All the houses are stone and nearly all open fires. No stoves at all. I really think everyone should have a open fire instead of a range, no nickel to polish. They make scones and oat cakes on a griddle. Tell the boys to think of the little boys and girls here. They can't buy chocolate bars or candy of any kind. They go all winter with their knees bare and no mittens on their hands. I want you to send me a pair of mittens for the winter for we feel the cold it is so damp here. I expect to get a letter from someone soon. There seems to be a lot of mail coming. But I will get mine someday soon. So Goodbye. Cheerio.

Also on that sailing were the other members of 15 Company who had passed basic training and medical boarding at Valcartier. Pat got to know most of the men over the next few years, and he wrote about many of them in his letters back home, passing on messages and news of their whereabouts. As the oldest recruit in the company, he became a father figure to the younger men, especially those he knew from home, like twenty-three-year-old Eddie O'Toole. Eddie's sister Eileen was married to Pat's oldest son, Roger, so he and Pat shared a family connection. On February 11, 1941, while on leave from Valcartier, Eddie had married in Bathurst. He and his bride Marion barely had time for a honeymoon before Eddie had to return to Quebec, only to be shipped off to Scotland with the rest of the company in April. Eddie was lonesome for his wife, and Pat kept a paternal eye on him, giving regular updates on the young man, which he knew would be passed on to the O'Tooles in Bathurst. "Well Eddie O'Toole is fine. He is on a truck now. I see the boy every day," he wrote on June 6, 1940. A couple of weeks later, Pat wrote to assure everyone that, unlike some of the other men who couldn't wait to get out of camp, Eddie didn't wander too far. This type of comment appeared frequently over the next few years: "Eddy [sic] O'Toole is just like an old man. He never leaves camp at all. He was disappointed he did not get a letter from his wife today. When you write he always asks if you speak of her."

Duncan Campbell was another man Pat knew from Bathurst, as were Locke Goneau of Tetagouche and Douglas Branch of Big River. Other familiar faces included Lawrence Riordon and Bedford Whelton from down shore. Then there were the new men Pat would get to know, including Zoel LaViolette of Nash Creek and Haywood Henry and his brother Robert "Bob" of Plaster Rock. Both the Henry brothers and LaViolette married war brides in Scotland, as did Charlie Gunning of Lower Jemseg and Arnett Cook of Saint John.

Among the others Pat referred to in his letters was Sergeant Fred Cogswell of Centreville, with whom Pat shared a bicycle for transportation. Little did Pat know that, after the war, Cogswell would go on to become one of Canada's foremost poets. The men were all living at such close quarters that, although they are not mentioned in his letters, Pat most certainly would also have known George Condley of Fredericton and the "Saw Doctor," Alfred Blizzard of Fredericton Junction. Blizzard's relationship with a young local

Eddie O'Toole was a good friend of Pat's from Bathurst, whose sister Eileen was married to Pat's eldest son Roger. Eddie went over to Scotland with Pat on the MS *Batory*.

(Photo courtesy of Marie (O'Toole) Roy)

woman from Kiltarlity was one of thousands between Canadian servicemen and single, British women that ended in heartbreak when, at the end of the war, the men were repatriated and left their girlfriends — and babies —behind.

The two hundred men who constituted the first overseas contingent of 15 Company were a cross-section of New Brunswick society: most were English speaking, of Irish, Scottish, or English ancestry with family ties to Britain. Others were more recent immigrants from the British Isles who were, in a sense, going home to familiar places where they still had family and friends. There were also French-speaking Acadians, whose ancestors had survived the Expulsion in 1755 to make a home for themselves in the new province of New Brunswick. The men of the company were from across the province, from coastal villages and riverside communities, the valleys and the highlands, and isolated rural areas where electricity and plumbing were still visions of the future. They had all survived the Depression years, some more scarred than the others, but all saw an opportunity in the Forestry Corps. They were high school and university-educated engineers, administrators, and skilled tradesmen in the forest industry who could command a decent wage in civilian life. They were also uneducated, illiterate, and low-paid loggers, who lived a hardscrabble existence following the seasonal employment of New Brunswick's natural resources economy, earning a pittance in the logging camps in winter and on the spring drive, and farming and fishing in the summer and fall—doing whatever they could to earn a living. Some were still in their teens, with logging experience earned on family woodlots; others were in their thirties, forties, and, in Pat's case, mid-fifties, whose entire working lives had been spent in the woods. Many were family men with teenaged children of their own—sons and daughters who would grow into young men and women while their father was overseas. Some 15 Company men had served in the First World War; others had joined the militia in the interwar years, bringing with them valuable military experience to an outfit that, although not expected to see any fighting in the Scottish Highlands, had to be prepared for battle should the Germans invade. Others had never donned a uniform in their lives, but were experienced fishers and hunters who knew how to shoot a rifle better than any soldier or commissioned officer. Single or married, rich or poor, young or middle aged, they were a diverse group from every corner of the province, and in all likelihood would never have met had it not been for the war. Circumstance threw them together on the MS *Batory* on a journey to a country that most knew little about.

That Easter Sunday, April 13, 1941, Mass was held in the first-class smoking saloon: it was the first Easter that any of the men had ever been to sea, and the services were well attended. Over the next five days, the boat rolled considerably, but, seasick or not, 15 Company was expected to fulfill sentry duties, both inside and on deck. On April 21, after ten days at sea, the unit disembarked at Gourock, forty-eight kilometres from Glasgow, and proceeded by train to Beauly, Inverness-shire, in the northern Scottish Highlands. There followed a ten-kilometre drive by lorry to Lovat No. 2 Camp at Boblainy Wood, where they arrived late at night, ate supper, and settled in. Next day, the New Brunswick lumbermen would see the place they would call home for the next three years.

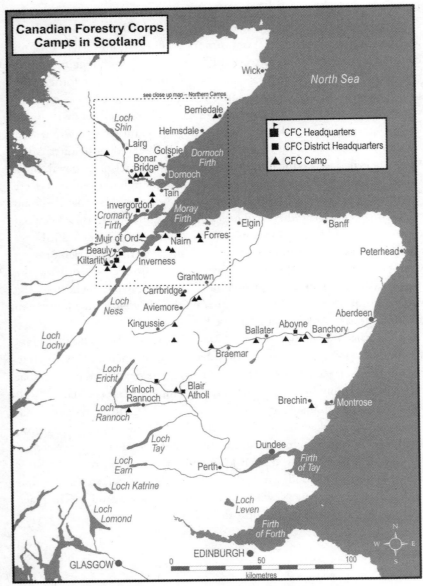

Canadian Forestry Corps Camps in Scotland

North Sea

Wick

see close up map – Northern Camps

Loch Shin

Berriedale

Helmsdale

Lairg

Golspie

Dornoch Firth

Bonar Bridge

Dornoch

■ CFC Headquarters
■ CFC District Headquarters
▲ CFC Camp

Tain

Invergordon

Cromarty Firth

Moray Firth

Muir of Ord

Nairn

Forres

Elgin

Banff

Beauly

Peterhead

Kiltarlity

Inverness

Grantown

Carrbridge

Aberdeen

Loch Ness

Aviemore

Kingussie

Ballater

Aboyne

Banchory

Loch Lochy

Braemar

Loch Ericht

Kinloch Rannoch

Blair Atholl

Brechin

Montrose

Loch Rannoch

Loch Tay

Loch Earn

Perth

Dundee

Firth of Tay

Loch Katrine

Loch Leven

Loch Lomond

Firth of Forth

N
W   E
S

GLASGOW

EDINBURGH

0   50   100
kilometres

Canadian Forestry Corps camps, Scotland (Mike Bechthold)

Chapter Three

Arrival in Scotland

It's unlikely that Pat Hennessy or any of the other ranks in 15 Company knew where they were going when they arrived dockside at Gourock, Scotland. That information would have been on a need-to-know basis, and even if the soldiers were told in the dark of night as they made their way to Boblainy Wood, outside Beauly, they must have wondered where they were in Scotland. Over the next few weeks, as the camp started taking shape and the men began venturing out into the little communities nearby, they would meet the locals and gain an appreciation of the people and history of the tiny Highland village of Beauly.

Beauly, Inverness-shire, is twenty kilometres west of Inverness, in the Scottish Highlands. During the war years, it had a population of a thousand, a number that is relatively unchanged today. A short distance south is the village of Kiltarlity, and farther west is Eskadale. The area is home to numerous clans, most notably the Fraser Lovats. The history of Beauly is closely tied to the Frasers, whose presence in England and Scotland dates back to the twelfth century. The first Simon Fraser was an adherent of William Wallace and Robert the Bruce. The second Simon Fraser fought at the Battle of Bannockburn in 1314. The Fraser Lovats have been connected to Beauly since 1367. Until 1995, when the castle and lands were sold to pay inheritance taxes, the Fraser family owned much of

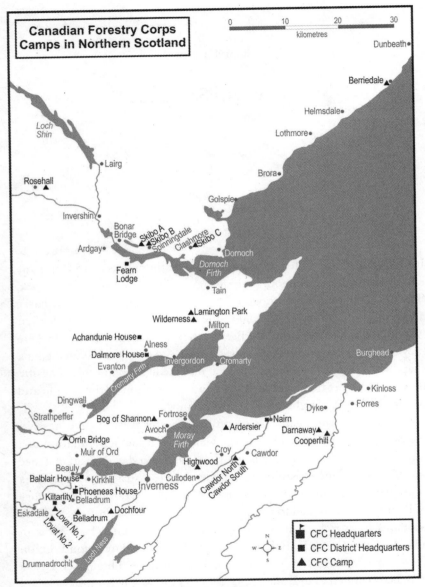

CFC camps in Northern Scotland (Mike Bechthold)

the surrounding property. The seat of the Fraser Lovats is Beaufort Castle. The original castle was established in 1511, but it was destroyed and then rebuilt a number of times over the centuries, lastly in 1880, when the 15th Lord Lovat commissioned the present building. Perched alongside the winding Beauly River, it stands today as a stunning example of red sandstone Scottish baronial architecture.

A short drive from Beauly is the Caledonian Canal and Loch Ness, site of thirteenth-century Urquhart Castle and "Nessie" — the mysterious and, some say, mythological Loch Ness Monster. "Nessie" was first sighted in 565 by Saint Columba as he was swimming in the freshwater loch. In 1933, the myth achieved celebrity status when a couple out for a drive reported seeing something resembling a whale in the water, leading to speculation and a growing tourism industry that persists to this day. Cawdor Castle, made famous by Shakespeare's Macbeth, is a short distance from Inverness, as is Culloden Moor, site of the bloodiest battle of the Jacobite Rebellion. The magical Clava Cairns, a Bronze Age burial site, is but two and a half kilometres from Culloden, and many Jacobites are believed to have passed through it as they made their escape from the battlefield.

The Catholic Fraser clan is famous for having supported Bonnie Prince Charlie in the 1745 Jacobite Rebellion. The clan's 11th Lord Lovat, also known as Simon Fraser, was among the Highland chiefs defeated on the Culloden battlefield. He was stripped of his titles and his castle, then known as "Dounie" Castle, was burned to the ground. Called "the most devious man in Scotland," Simon Fraser was the last man in Britain to be beheaded publicly, for treason in 1747 at Tower Hill in London. Nearly two hundred years later, another Simon Fraser, "Shimi," the 17th Lord Lovat and 25th chief of the Clan Fraser, was commanding officer of No. 4 Commando in the abortive Dieppe raid of August 19, 1942. A handsome, swashbuckling character right out of central casting, Lovat earned the admiration of Winston Churchill, who, in a letter to Josef Stalin, called Lovat "the mildest-mannered man that ever scuttled a ship or cut a throat." At Dieppe, Lovat earned a Distinguished Service Order (DSO) for successfully attacking and destroying his target of six 150 mm guns. In so doing, the famed commandos became one of the few units to complete their mission in what is considered Canada's darkest day of the Second World War. On D-Day, Lord Lovat, then brigadier and commander of the newly formed 1st Special Service Brigade, was famously piped onto Sword Beach at Normandy in defiance of specific orders not to do so in battle. The scene was immortalized in the Hollywood film *The Longest Day*, with Lovat played by English actor Peter Lawford. As the story goes, when Lovat's faithful piper, Bill Millin, reminded the brigadier of the order, Lovat said, "Ah, but that's the English ar Office. You and I are both Scottish, and that doesn't apply."

Beauly village square, described as the "most spacious in northern Scotland," was laid out by the 13th Lord Lovat in 1840, and sits on the edge of historic Beauly Priory. Built by the Valliscaulian Order of the Benedictine monks in 1230, the priory is fringed by trees and framed by wooded hills. It was once visited by Mary Queen of Scots, who is said to have given the area its name, "Beauly," or "Beautiful place," although in reality the name had been around before she arrived. Over the centuries, the priory fell into ruin and only the Abbey Church, roofless but with its medieval burial tombs and graveyard largely intact, has survived into the twenty-first century. In April 1941, when the Canadians arrived, the priory would have looked very much like it had for five centuries — quite a sight for men from the New World, whose idea of old buildings would have been at most 150 years.

It was into this remote Highland setting that the men of 15 Company found themselves in April 1941. With the war in the forefront of everyone's mind, most knew little of the ten thousand years of pre-history surrounding them: of Mesolithic arrowheads, Neolithic and Bronze Age burial cairns and standing stones, Iron Age crannogs, and a long-lost Pictish kingdom, so named by the Romans, who, it is claimed, never made it as far north as Beauly. They would learn of medieval churches and castles, and of twentieth-century lords and ladies who were part of everyday life in Scotland. But all that exploring could wait until the New Brunswickers had built a Canadian-style logging camp in the remote forest of Lord Lovat's Boblainy Wood. The wood is located ten kilometres south of Beauly, and four kilometres back in the hills from Kiltarlity. Boblainy was one small

Beaufort Castle, Beauly, the ancestral home of Lord Lovat. On special occasions during the war, Lady Lovat invited Roman Catholics among the Canadians to attend Mass at the private chapel; Pat was one of the lucky few to have gone more than once.

part of the huge Lovat Estate in Inverness-shire that had been turned over to the British government for the duration of the wartime emergency.

The 16th Lord Lovat, the famed Shimi's father, was a leader in the scientific development of Scotland's forests. As former head of the Forestry Commission, Lovat had spent a considerable amount of his own wealth on the family's land holdings since 1909. By the time war broke out in 1939, the 16th Lord Lovat was gone, the title having passed on to Shimi. But the vast woodlands that Shimi's father preserved and the new ones he planted around Beauly and Kiltarlity were ready for harvest. The Lovats, along with many other estate owners throughout the Highlands, threw their support and forests behind the war effort.

Of the thirty CFC camps in Scotland, six were located near Beauly under the jurisdiction of No. 5 District Headquarters, which commanded 6,

10, 15, 18, 19, and 21 Companies. Two companies were based on the Lovat Estate itself: 15 Company, at Lovat No. 2 at Boblainy Wood, and a British Columbia unit, 18 Company from Victoria, at Lovat No. 1 (also known as Teanacoil Camp), two and a half kilometres southwest of Kiltarlity, between Teanacoil Wood and Femnock Wood. Reinforcing its connection to the Lovat Estate, in July 1941, No. 5 District Headquarters moved operations to Balblair House, a large "dower house" built in 1800 for the widow, or "dowager," of the estate owner. Balblair House was a two-storey stone building with an imposing driveway and landscaped gardens that would have been a major step up from Lovat No. 1, in which No. 5 District Headquarters had been operating since arriving in Scotland in April. Combined with CFC Headquarters at Phoineas House in Belladrum, and Edmonton-based 19 Company operations nearby, Beauly became a busy hub of CFC operations in Scotland, and the Lovat Estate was at the centre of the entire forestry scheme.

Typical of CFC operations in Scotland, 15 and 18 Companies worked the same area, with 15 Company cutting the bush and bringing out the timber, and 18 Company sawing it into lumber at the Canadian-built sawmill at Kiltarlity, using mostly Canadian mechanical equipment. In an article about the CFC that appeared in the *Canadian Geographical Journal* in 1944, Canadian historian (and later lieutenant governor of New Brunswick) George Stanley described the Scottish setting: "Each company was a largely self-contained unit. It operates its own bush gang and its own mill. It [carried] on its strength tradesmen of every kind necessary for the efficient carrying on of its allotted task; sawyers, millwrights, mechanics, lumberjacks, camp cooks, electricians, shoemakers, tailors, carpenters, and so forth. It has its own armourer sergeant, its military instructors and its medical orderlies. It has its own garages and workshops. Each camp is planned on similar lines and provided with standardized equipment."

Within twenty-four hours of arrival at Lovat No. 2 on April 21, 1941, the men of 15 Company were hard at work. The soil was quite boggy and needed considerable draining, a job civilian contractors already had under way. Although they had a good water supply, toilet facilities and water for washing and showers were unavailable, so all ranks used rather "primitive conveniences" until the necessary facilities could be built. There had been a mix-up, and much of 15 Company's technical equipment was sent in error to 18 Company at Teanacoil. This necessitated extra haulage and negotiation to get 15 Company's stores redirected. Over the following weeks, the men were divided into crews, one to ditch a road through the camp and build a culvert, another to clear the woods and put a quarter-mile road through from the camp to the main road as well as eliminate several bad turns.

Still another crew was tasked with cleaning up the aftermath of a well-intentioned, but failed, experiment by the Ministry of Supply's Home Grown Timber Production Department (formerly called the Forestry Commission). Despite the urgent need for professional foresters and loggers in Scotland, most had joined the services, and were now gainfully employed in the army, navy, and air force. Given the war emergency, the government tapped into unskilled civilian labour—school boys and university graduates—who left behind a mess of logs at Boblainy that required quite a bit of work by 15 Company to untangle. As the war diary noted, "A large number of trees had been cut and apparently little attempt had been made to get the cut out. As most of the cut was on a steep side hill, and there was no suitable road to the operation, the trees were left where they were felled, with the exception of a small number of logs which had been hauled to a field back of No. 15 COY. The trees had been felled in every direction and presented plenty in the way of difficulties when work was started in getting them out."

While the loggers sorted out the Ministry of Supply experiment, Lieutenant Edgar Hanson, a civil engineer from Fredericton, surveyed a three-mile logging road from Lovat No. 2 to the tract of timber to be cut by 15 Company, a task that continued through to May. That month, construction began at the sawmill at Kiltarlity, and by the end of May the first logging began. 15 Company's war diarist recorded that the sawmill was "expected to be the largest in Scotland," processing the wood cut by 15 and 18 Companies at Lovat No. 1 and No. 2. In a few weeks, the men of 15 Company had accomplished a great deal. Turning an isolated forest into a working camp site with running water, roads, and the beginning of a sawmill was no small feat.

Company's camp at Boblainy Wood, on the Lovat Estate

Although the Canadians had come to Scotland to cut wood, they were also a military unit of the army. "Whether or not the men approve," wrote the war diarist, it was important they receive military training in the event of a German invasion. To that effect, in mid-May instructions directed that a "certain amount of training" would take place on Saturday afternoons. Everyone understood the necessity of being prepared for an enemy attack, but even though they had been at Lovat No. 2 for nearly a month, arms had yet to be delivered. Among the entire company, they had only three pistols, with ammunition belonging to officers who had brought them to Scotland from Canada. The difficulty of training without rifles was solved somewhat on May 22, when a shipment of 153 Lee-Enfield rifles and bayonets arrived. Unfortunately, the men had been trained on Ross rifles at Camp Valcartier and, in addition to a lack of ammunition, no syllabus was provided — although it did arrive, along with the ammunition, at the end of the month.

In what is the first of many observations to appear throughout 15 Company's war diary over the next five years, one can sense the bewilderment and frustration at the plodding military bureaucracy. Most, if not all, of the officers were university-educated foresters and industry professionals who had come from the private sector. Although some had military experience in the militia or even in the First World War, and were used to dealing with isolation and foul-ups, the irony of a rifle without bullets and no instructions was too much for this war diarist to ignore: "It seems to be a good rifle, although no ammunition is available. No doubt we shall receive ammunition. Soon, we hope." Ammunition finally arrived in mid-June, and by this time the Kiltarlity mill was running. What Pat Hennessy thought of all the administrative problems is unknown: his job as camp cook kept him occupied from sunup to sundown preparing breakfast, dinner, and supper every day for the logging crews, who were working very hard building the roads and sawmill that spring.

Other than their basic training at Valcartier, most of the loggers had little or no military experience, and frequently had to be cautioned on the basics of army discipline. Living in camps for weeks and months on end, they saw little reason for saluting or wearing uniforms properly. The majority of CFC men were professional outdoorsmen, having worked and lived in logging camps most of their adult lives. It's unlikely they had ever seen such a carefully managed estate, where a games keeper, or "Ghillie," looked after the deer and salmon for private sport. The Canadians were fascinated by the abundance of fish and game on the Lovat Estate, but the lands and rivers belonged to Lord Lovat. Complaints about CFC men skipping rocks on the Beauly River led to the first of many Routine Orders about disturbing the wildlife that must have raised a few hackles in the camp.

Part I Orders
30 May, 1941
Beauly River

Attention has been drawn to the fact that other ranks of the CFC have been throwing stones and other articles into the Beauly River. As this is a privately owned salmon river, the practice indulged in is detrimental to the fishing and must cease forthwith.

Should the above mentioned practice continue, not only will disciplinary action be taken against the offenders, but it will be necessary to place the walks on the banks of the Beauly River and vicinity out of bounds.

(H.R. Currie) Lieut. and Adjt.

Poaching was another temptation that many Canadians found too difficult to resist, especially when they had the help of locals who were also suspected of ignoring the Scottish sporting rights of the upper class. Throughout the various CFC war diaries are references to good fishing on various estates, as well as complaints about poaching salmon; yet only one complaint about CFC personnel poaching game was recorded, and it wasn't about 15 Company. That didn't mean more complaints weren't received: the issue was serious enough that, in March 1943, CFC Headquarters declared "severe disciplinary action" against poachers as a matter of "national food interest." Under the title, "Poaching, Prevention of," the following order was announced to 15 Company: "Severe disciplinary action will be taken against anyone convicted of poaching game. With the approach of the breeding season, it is essential in the national food interest that such practices be stopped. Formation and Unit Commanders will ensure that this Order is brought to the notice of All Ranks."

In the end, enforcement proved to be as difficult to implement as it would have been to stop the Canadians from looking at the deer and other wildlife that were so plentiful on the Lovat Estate. "The deer look good and fat here now," Pat observed in a letter to Bea just two months after arriving in Scotland. In Canada he would have shot the animal and served it up for dinner, but in Scotland the rules were different. That December Pat wrote about the hunting to his son Bunny (James), who at age nineteen was already an experienced woodsman: "James the deer are awful thick here but we aren't allowed to hunt them. They are bigger than our deer. They have a small one they call a Roe Deer that only weigh 35 lbs dressed.

The deer roar here or call in the mating season. They make a noise like a hungry calf bawling. I have heard them often. This fall they are cross, believe me. They are the only thing here in Scotland that would tackle you and I don't believe they would do much either. There are lots of grouse, pheasants, partridge and spruce partridge."

Fortunately, there were plenty of grey rabbits in Scotland that could be shot, trapped, or snared legally. Before the war, rabbit would have been a rare main dish for the Scots, but with strict rationing in force, rabbits were now a luxury on par with chicken. In camp, however, the loggers ate well, with supplies sourced mainly from the Canadian Army. In June, Pat informed Bea: "I get plenty to eat. We have bacon and eggs, beans, sausages and the best of beef. Cabbage, carrots, turnips and jam—the best jam I ever tasted. All kinds of berries, blackberry, raspberries, gooseberries, black currants and a dozen more." Pat could grow at least two crops of lettuce in the little vegetable garden he sowed, but a reliable source of eggs and milk required a visit to local farmers. It was through Pat's ventures out to Beauly for supplies that he was introduced to the workers on the Lovat Estate, including blacksmith Don Fraser and his wife Hannah. Through them he met Father Aeonas Geddes, the Roman Catholic priest at St. Mary's, Eskadale, and the most prominent Catholic families in the district, including the dowager, Lady Laura, her son "Shimi," the 17th Lord Lovat, and his wife, Lady Rosamund.

John and Annie Mackie, a Scots-Irish couple
Pat met at church in Edinburgh

Chapter Four

Meeting the Locals

Don Fraser and I went for a drive last night. We were to Lord Lovat's castle. It was wonderful. The statue of the Blessed Virgin is over the main door. It is wonderful to see.
— Patrick Hennessy to Beatrice Hennessy, June 17, 1941

That year in Scotland, Pat and the men of 15 Company saw many firsts, from meeting the locals and getting accustomed to the weather and the unique culture of the Highlands to travelling throughout Scotland and England and seeing the places they had heard so much about. After three weeks in camp, Pat went on his first privileged leave, departing on May 6 for Edinburgh, the ancient capital city of Scotland. Along with Pat on the trip were two cooks and Bathurst friends Locke Goneau from Tetagouche and Douglas Branch from Big River.

Pat was clearly enamoured with the beauty of the city, its wide streets, and modern shops with their famous Scotch tweeds. A devout Catholic, he even attended mass at St. Mary's Cathedral on York Street, which was a small church by New Brunswick standards. "I was at mass yesterday at the cathedral, a small little church. All the three priests are from Ireland." While in Edinburgh, Pat met a Scots-Irish Roman Catholic couple named John and Annie Mackie. John was a manager at the Chancelot Flour Mill in Leith and Annie ran two grocery stores (called "press agents") in Portabello and Craigentinny. Pat returned to the Mackies' many times over the next few years. and they graciously welcomed him back to their comfortable bungalow, introducing him to their wide circle of friends in business and theatre. After Pat's second trip to Edinburgh in 1942, Annie wrote to Bea in New Brunswick, explaining who she was and how much they enjoyed meeting "Mr. Hennessy."

May 25, 1942
Dear Mrs. Hennessy:

My husband and I are strangers to you, I know, but we both wish you to realize how pleased we have been to meet Mr. Hennessy and whenever he is in Edinburgh he can always come down to visit us. There is always an open door to him and he will feel he has some friends here. I know we can never make him feel or miss the loss of yourself and the family but this is just our wee bit towards what you Canadians are doing for us.

God is good and I hope with God's help we will have peace soon and all together again as of old.

Kindest regards to all of you.

Yours sincerely,
Anne Mackie

Before Pat left for that first trip to Edinburgh, he had met Don and Hannah Fraser, a middle-aged couple with whom he became very close friends during his nearly five years in Scotland. In the Frasers Pat found a substitute family in Beauly who opened their doors and hearts to the Canadians. As many Scots did during the Second World War, Don's wife Hannah offered to write to Pat's family in Bathurst, thus beginning a correspondence between Scotland and Canada that lasted the rest of their lives. In one of Pat's first letters to his daughter Anna, written from Edinburgh on May 12, 1941, Pat asks if Bea has received Mrs. Fraser's first letter yet: "A family, Mr. and Mrs. Fraser was going to write to Momma. Did she get it? They have 2 boys one 10-14. They are lovely people."

Don Fraser was the blacksmith at the Lovat Estate. He and Hannah and their two sons Simon and William lived in Old Downie, a row of two-storey stone cottages located a short distance from Beaufort Castle. The name "Downie" was a nod to the original "Castle Dounie," which

Hannah Fraser, sons William and Simon, with Pat Hennessy and Jimmy Cameron of 15 Company outside the Fraser home at Old Downie, Beauly

sat on the site of Beaufort Castle in the 1100s, three hundred years before the Frasers of Lovat became the area's principal landowners. Old Downie was a self-contained community of workers who spent their working lives on the estate, passing on their jobs and housing from one generation to the next. At Old Downie, Hannah kept a vegetable garden, a goat for milk, and a few chickens and laying hens. By the end of the war, her menagerie had expanded to include two goats, thirty-three chickens, and fifty-five laying hens, whose eggs she could sell to registered dealers.

In one of her first letters to Bea, Hannah Fraser explains how a great Scottish estate worked.

> You were asking if we had a farm. No my husband is a black-smith on a private estate. That is — in Scotland there are great parts of land owned by a landlord and it is inheritable property going down to the oldest son. Lord Lovat, the great

Commando leader, owns Beaufort Estate and Castle and that's where we live. No, not at the castle but on the Estate, and my husband is blacksmith for the place. He just gets a weekly wage as it is private and doesn't do outside work.

The present Laird's father died since we came here. The present one was just 21, that's ten years ago. He married four years ago and had a son, an heir, a few days before war was declared. As is the custom when an heir is born we had a huge bonfire near the castle and there were great celebrations. They have two girls born since. I will send you a photo of the castle some time but maybe Pat has sent you one. They are a Roman Catholic family and Pat sees them at chapel and he will be able to tell you all about them when he goes home. Lovat is the chief of the Clan Fraser so we have the name all right. Simon is the great family name but my Simon's name comes from the other side of the family. I was brought up on a small holding or croft and know all there is to know about the work. We have a big garden here and we have all our vegetables. Pat loves to get a fresh taste especially a few potatoes. I just wish when I mix the surplus for the year I could pass them on to someone who would enjoy them. They all say they are to bring back a few seed so Scotland will be mixed in all sorts of ways with Canada Scotch both right enough.

Pat's network of friends spread throughout the Fraser family. Don's older brother John Lee Fraser and his wife Alice lived at Bonnyview, a small hill croft high up the glen at Ruisaurie, overlooking the village and winding Beauly River. John Lee had also worked at Beaufort Castle and lived at Old Downie, but when he retired, he and Alice took over his parents' croft at Bonnyview. Below, in the rolling hills, was a captivating view of Beaufort Castle and the river, which pours into Beauly Firth. John Lee and Alice had three children, Murdo, Catherine, and Nan, who were young adults with families of their own when Pat met their parents during the war. John Lee and Alice were closer in age to Pat than were Don and Hannah Fraser,

The scene from Bonnyview, the home of John Lee and Alice Fraser, in the hills above Beauly with a commanding view of Beaufort Castle and Beauly Firth (Photo by the author)

and Pat spent many happy days with them at Bonnyview when he had time off from camp. Pat even visited with their daughter Nan Munro and her young family in Ayr, spending time touring the Scottish countryside with Nan's husband Alec, who worked as a travelling salesman after being released from the military due to stomach problems.

As Pat soon found out, the "Lee-Frasers" of Beauly descended from the "boll of meal" Frasers, whose original name was Lee. During the time of Simon "The Fox" Fraser—the Jacobite who was executed by the English after the disaster at Culloden—tenants were offered a "boll" of meal to change their name in order to increase the number of the clan. "A boll of meal, about eight stone [nearly 51 kilograms], was a valuable household commodity in those days and not to be miffed at!" explained Kenneth A. McCrae, a local author who wrote about John Lee Fraser in his 1953 book *Highland Doorstep*. "John Lee Fraser is not ashamed to own up to being 'a boll of meal Fraser'," wrote McCrae.

In meeting the Frasers, Pat was fulfilling one of Bea's wishes: to solve the mystery of her Scottish-born great-grandfather, Alexander Fraser. Oral history passed down through Bea's family held that Alexander was born in "Fraserville" in 1799. He emigrated to Canada as a young man, and after the Great Miramichi Fire of 1825, he walked all the way to Bathurst, marrying Anamelia Shipman Grant of Dunlop in 1831. Alexander was Presbyterian and Anamelia was Roman Catholic. As was the practice in the mid-nineteenth century, the five children were raised in their mother's faith. One of the children, Nancy, born in 1837, was Bea's grandmother, and Bea remembered Nancy's saying that Alexander was from an area around the Caledonian Canal. All the original birth, marriage, and death certificates, as well as any correspondence, were burned in a fire at the old Fraser homestead in Tetagouche at the turn of the twentieth century. Making the story suspect is the fact that there is no place called "Fraserville," but there is a Fraserburgh, near Aberdeen. It might have been wishful thinking, but it's also possible that "Fraserville" refers to Beauly, the ancestral home of Clan Fraser. Pat assumed, as did many other Canadians overseas during the war, that tracing an ancestor in Scotland would be easy. Not so. Even with his new-found Fraser friends in Beauly, Pat never did find Alexander, but it wasn't for lack of trying. One can imagine him in the land of the Frasers, asking everyone he met if they knew an Alexander who went to New Brunswick, Canada, in the early 1800s. Still, Don and Hannah took Pat's inquiries about Alexander Fraser very seriously. By June 25, 1941, Hannah had already written two letters to "Mrs. Hennessy," going into great detail to explain the possible connections Alexander might have had with the Beauly area: "You will see the Caledonian Canal runs quite close to us here and it is very likely the one your Grandmother spoke of. If you could give us the name of the place we might be able to trace them. Mr. Hennessy thinks the name is on the monument in the cemetery. Lots of the old folks left records in Bibles. It would be nice to trace them up." The Frasers were Protestant adherents of the Church of Scotland, but it made little difference to Pat. In New Brunswick religion divided people. but in Beauly what they shared as friends in the midst of a terrible war was more important. Besides, Don Fraser and Father Aeonas Geddes,

Lawrence Riordon of Riordon, NB, and Bedford Whelton of Black Rock, NB, good friends of Pat's in 15 Company, having sailed with him to Scotland in April 1941. Both volunteered for No. 1 Canadian Forestry Group, and served in Northwest Europe from July 1944 to the end of hostilities in May 1945. Lawrence saw action in the Ardennes at Christmas 1944, when he was told to "throw down his axe and pick up a rifle."

the Lovat family's personal chaplain who also served as parish priest at St. Mary's, Eskadale, went salmon fishing together. Pat soon joined Don and Father Geddes fishing for salmon at the priest's home on Beauly River, the trio bridging a gap in religion and class that would have seemed inconceivable back in Canada. It was through fishing that Pat and Father Geddes got to know each other, using salmon flies sent to Scotland by Lucy's husband Sidney, who was a professional salmon fly tyer himself. Religion and attendance at church also connected Pat and the other soldiers with the local community. So close were the Catholic CFC men to the friendly Scottish priest that they became known, affectionately, as "Father Geddes's Boys." In a letter to his daughter Anna, Pat describes Father Geddes and speaks of the kindness of the Scots, Catholic and Protestant: "I am getting some snaps of Lawrence Riordon and I taken with Father Geddes, a Scotch Priest at the church we go to. He takes us in and gives us a cup of tea after mass. Everyone seems so good and kind. The Frasers gave me a nice feather pillow."

Pat also attended services at St. Mary's Catholic Church in Beauly, a red sandstone chapel built in 1864 with the financial support of the 14th Lord Lovat. It was a six-mile walk to St. Mary's on Sunday, and Pat made the trek often because, according to him, the camps were not a priority for the army's Catholic chaplains. In a letter to Bea in late June 1941, Pat complains about the lack of church services for Catholics: "Well Bee we have 6 miles to go to church. Our chaplain only came once in to the camps. I don't know where he keeps himself. The English minister comes every second Sunday. They don't have any church parade at all." The upside was that Pat befriended the parish priest at St. Mary's, Father George Grant, and over the next four years Pat became a regular at both St. Mary's, Beauly, and at St. Mary's, Eskadale, with Father Geddes. Through these churches, Pat met Catholic families such as the Campbells, Morrisons, Chisholms, and Johnstones, some of whom took up letter writing to Canada that survived long after the war.

In 1944, Pat even stood in as best man at the marriage of CFC man Edward "Ed" Pallot to Margaret Fraser Rose — an interesting event because of what it says about the importance of religion back in Canada. Pat met Ed Pallot when the thirty-four-year-old accountant was transferred from 4 Company in Aboyne, near Ballater. Ed became the pay sergeant for the No. 5 District at Beauly, and the two men likely became friends through their attendance at St. Mary's, Beauly. Ed was a Catholic from Montreal and his wife Margaret, a Scottish war bride from Aboyne, was Protestant. The couple was actually married at St. Machar's (Church of Scotland) in Aboyne in 1941, and they had a daughter Rosalind, who was born in December 1943. The Catholic/Protestant mix wasn't a problem in Scotland, but it most certainly would be in Catholic Montreal, where the couple intended to live after the war. In fall 1944, they decided it would be in the family's best interest for Margaret and Rosalind to convert. In order for that to happen, the couple had to get married again, this time in the Catholic Church, essentially erasing the existence of the previous marriage. Meantime, little Rosalind would have to be baptized as well. On September 24, 1944, Edward and Margaret were married at St. Mary's, Beauly, by Father Grant, and Rosalind was baptized. At both events, Pat

CERTIFICATE OF MARRIAGE.

I Certify *that, according to the Register of Marriages kept at this Church,* St.MARY's BEAULY Edward Pallot *and* Margaret Rose *were* **Married** *at the above Church by Rev.* George Grant P.P. *according to the Rites of the Catholic Church, on the* 24 Sept th. *day of* September 1944 *in the presence of* P.J.Hennessy (5 District HQ C.F.C.) *and* Lily Johnstone of Beauly

Given the 26th *day of* October 1944

for Rev. George Canon Grant P.P.
Fr. J.M.A. Mornet (Military Chaplain)

Chaplain (R.C.)

Pat Hennessy and Lily Johnstone of Beauly were witnesses to the Roman Catholic wedding of Ed and Margaret (Rose) Pallot in September 1944. The Pallots were actually married three years earlier in the Church of Scotland, but they decided it would be best to get married again in the Catholic Church before leaving for Canada. (Courtesy of Rosalind (Pallot) Pett)

and Lily Johnstone of Beauly stood in as witnesses to these most ancient rites of the Catholic Church.

As spring turned into summer, Pat used every break he got from the kitchen to explore the countryside on his bicycle, writing glowing letters back home to his family about the people he met and the places he discovered in the area surrounding Beauly. From the very beginning, he included slips of purple heather and brightly coloured flower blossoms, affixing them firmly to the top of his letters with sticky strips of white paper that still hold fast today. Pat also began a habit of inserting documents containing bits of news from the camp, newspapers, ticket stubs, forms, receipts, photos, and cards from his many trips to Edinburgh, Stirling, Glasgow, London, Manchester, and eventually Ireland. These archival documents were then carefully tucked away by Bea back in Bathurst, some of them making their way into a scrapbook about Pat's experiences that started in December 1940, but then grew to include news about their sons Roger, James, and Bruno, all of whom joined the armed services. As one

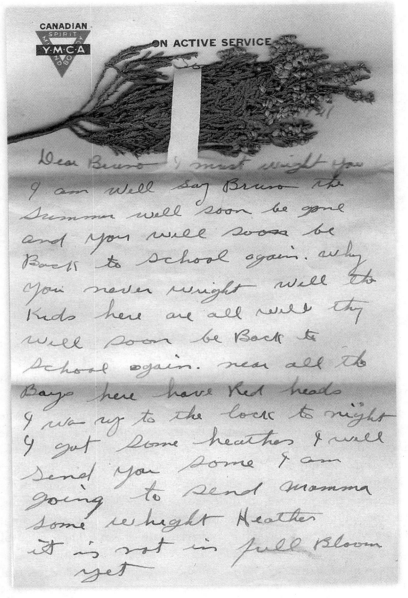

Dear Bruno I must wright you
I am Well Say Bruno the
Summer well soon be gone
and you will soon be
Back to school again. Why
you never wright Well the
Kids here are all well they
will soon be Back to
school again. near all the
Boys here have Red heads
I wa up to the locks to night
I got some heather I will
send you some I am
going to send mamma
some wehight Heather
it is not in full Bloom
yet

Letter from Pat to Bruno with snip of heather attached; after nearly
seventy-five years, the heather is still as bright as the day it was picked.

scrapbook filled up, another began, and by war's end there were more than a half-dozen, filled to the brim with news of the war's progress from the pages of the Saint John *Telegraph Journal*, Bathurst *Northern Light*, Toronto *Star Weekly*, and *Montreal Gazette*. Included among the many articles were stories of Norway's role in the conflict, a nod to Anna's beau Henrik Wesenberg, whom Pat would eventually meet in Scotland during the war.

In one of his early letters to Bea, Pat combines observations of nature with requests for a few things he can't get in Scotland, and ends with news of a promotion to officers' cook.

> Bee the country is so beautiful now. One can't tell you. You will have to come and see it for yourself. I was out to the lake today fishing. We did not have very good luck. My the lakes are nice. They are all crowded with flowing bushes and pond lilies. There is a bush that flowers. The flower is like a peonie rose only hardy and the leaf is like a bay leaf. There is three different colours, pink, lavender, white. Then there is another, a yellow bush flower called the broom tree. The flower is like sweet pea. It has been in bloom since April and keeps blooming all summer. The horse chestnut is just loaded with blossoms.
>
> If you want to send any thing candy of any kind chocolate bars, we can't get any and if you have any summer savory send a little, we can't get any here.
>
> I cook for the officers now and a dozen men.

In May, during his first visit to Edinburgh, Pat was interviewed along with a number of men from 15 Company by the Canadian Army Photo and Film Unit for radio broadcast in Canada on the CBC. The short "messages from troops" were a morale booster intended to be a living link between the Canadian forces and the people back home. Pat's message was probably intended for broadcast in the lead-up to Dominion Day on July 1. In late June, Pat wrote to his daughter Lucy, eager to know if she had heard him yet on the radio in Canada. In another letter written to Bea in the first week of July, he asks again if anyone had heard the broadcast: "Did you hear me on the radio? I was on a short time ago. I was in hopes you would be listening in. There was one from each town spoke, Fredericton, Chatham, Newcastle, Woodstock etc." It took until February 1942 before Pat found out whether anyone in Bathurst had heard him on the radio broadcast. Like so many of his questions that were never answered, he finally gave up asking.

Perhaps the answer was to be found in one of the many letters lost during the Battle of the Atlantic, the prolonged struggle between the Allies and Germans for control of the Atlantic that began in 1939 and only ended with the conclusion of hostilities in 1945. Safely tucked away in the Highlands of Scotland, Pat could only observe the growing concerns of the people around him and pass on his fervent wish that the war would soon be over so he could see his family again: "Anna you must write often. I miss you all so much and if I do not get to see you again, remember me to all."

Chapter Five

England and the Search for Mrs. Haggerty

The people in Scotland are nicer than London.
— Patrick Hennessy to Beatrice Hennessy, September 14, 1941

At the end of August 1941, Pat went on his second privileged leave, this time on his own to London and Aldershot, where he sought out relatives, hoping to see his nephews: Weaver, son of his brother George from Blackville, as well as Edison, Elbridge, and Hubert (Cayo) Hennessy, the sons of his brother William. William Hennessy had moved to Campbellton from the family farm on Howard Road in Blackville at the turn of the century, married, and raised a family. Now Pat's four nephews were in England, and he could hardly wait to see them. But Pat was disappointed with his first trip south to Aldershot: the Hennessy boys had been moved, and the military wouldn't say where. In a letter to Lucy some months later, Cayo wrote about the mix-up: "Was sorry to know that Uncle Pat had been to see me and I had moved. But at the time, I was only 15 miles from my former camp."

Even if he didn't see his nephews, Pat's trip to England wasn't a complete waste of time. He was pleased to see some familiar faces from the North Shore (New Brunswick) Regiment, especially Father Myles Hickey, a young priest from Jacquet River. Father Hickey had been the popular curate at Sacred Heart parish in Bathurst in the mid-1930s and was well known to the Hennessy family. At Sacred Heart Academy, where Lucy and Anna received a private high school education, Father Hickey was a frequent

The Scarlet Dawn

THE

SCARLET DAWN

By

Msgr. R. M. Hickey,

Major, M.C.

In this story you have the
periences of a well-known C
adian Army Chaplain, wh
personality was the inspira
of many a soldier during
past war.

You will like this story, fo
is told with that touch of hu
and understanding that
deared the author to the tro
and made him the most
spected and best beloved
Chaplains.

UNIPRESS

Pat's son Roger drew the cover art for Father Myles Hickey's
wartime memoir, *The Scarlet Dawn*. (Author's collection)

visitor. At times, he could even be convinced to sing "Rose Of Tralee" to the
students, all girls, who, according to Lucy, would make him blush with their
giggling. After the war, Father Hickey wrote *The Scarlet Dawn*, the story of
his service with the North Shore Regiment and considered one of the most
important Canadian memoirs of the Second World War. The book was so
popular that it sold out and was reprinted many times, the last in 1980.

In Aldershot, Pat also saw Harry Hachey, Bruno Branch, Cecil Black,
and Harold Christie from Bathurst, and he said they seemed surprised

to see him. But mostly he was on his own. In London, he went on a tour of Westminster Abbey, walked under the famed Marble Arch, and, while admitting there were some nice buildings, he seemed unimpressed with Buckingham Palace and Petticoat Lane, preferring Edinburgh to London. The loud and boisterous shopping district in the East End, where Jewish merchants shouted out and hawked their wares on the sidewalks, seemed "funny" to Pat, who knew several Jewish store owners in Bathurst, including the Dalfens, Holdengrabers, and Moe Dingott, who sold high fashion women's clothing from Montreal.

Dear Bee:

Well I don't like London. It is too crowded and flat. But they had some lovely buildings and some nice ones left. Buckingham Palace isn't so nice as you think it to be. One will be disappointed when you see it. I was through Petticoat Lane, all Jews there selling on the street. All their clothing racks are out of their stores. It looks funny.

Well the old Temple is all Blitzed. What a shame. I got a piece of the marble for a souvenir. I got a book on Westminster Cathedral. I will send it to you.

Say Bee, all the parks are not kept up at all in London. One didn't find them nice at all not like Edinburgh. Well Edinburgh is swell now. All the flowers of the season are in full bloom now. I was to Portabello to the seaside. It is quite nice but not like the Points. The beach is rough, but what a crowd.

It was during this time that Pat made his first attempt to find Mrs. Cecilia Haggerty in Manchester. Cecilia Haggerty (née Worthington) was an Englishwoman the Hennessys met in Bathurst in the 1920s. "Cissie," as she was known, married a local farmer, Augustine Haggerty of Tetagouche, but returned to England in 1928 under tragic circumstances. Although the families corresponded for several years, there had been no letters since

1936, when Cissie married James Bird of Manchester. All Pat had was an outdated mailing address and orders from Beatrice to find the woman.

Cissie met Augustine Haggerty through pen pals, a popular form of communication in the early 1920s, when writing letters was practically an art form. At the time, the forty-year-old bachelor farmer was living in North Tetagouche, a small community settled by Irish Catholic immigrants in the 1800s. Haggerty's father, Daniel, had come over in 1847 during the Famine, settling in North Tetagouche and raising a family there. Twenty-four-year old Cissie, meantime, was living with her parents in Manchester. She was an only child, and no one knows what Cissie's parents thought of her Canadian pen pal, but in 1921 Augustine proposed marriage, and she said yes.

On November 6, 1921, Cissie arrived in Halifax on board the SS *Scythia*, and was married to Augustine at Pier 2 the same day. One month later, another young Englishwoman, Ethel Rumfitt, also came to North Tetagouche to marry Patrick O'Kane. The Haggertys and O'Kanes in North Tetagouche, and Beatrice's relatives in South Tetagouche, the Kanes (not related), were friends. It wasn't long before the two Englishwomen befriended Beatrice, visiting with their young children at the Hennessy family homestead in Bathurst when they came into town for church services. Unfortunately, the Haggerty marriage did not last long. Rumour was that Augustine had a reputation for being jealous and abusive of Cissie and the three children, Margaret (born 1923), Roland (born 1924), and Norman (born 1927). Even the farm animals were afraid of Augustine. On one of her visits, Cissie confided to Beatrice that she was not allowed to talk to the neighbours, and as punishment he had locked her and the children in a room to prevent them from leaving.

On the night of December 29, 1927, Augustine was coming home from a night of drinking when he stumbled trying to get off his wagon. This startled the horse, which was already skittish around the farmer. The animal ran off with Augustine's foot caught in the wheel, dragging the man some distance. Augustine's leg had to be amputated. Patrick O'Kane, who was known locally as a "horse whisperer," came to the house, caught up with the animal, and calmed him down. But it was too late for Augustine: gangrene set in, and by January 11, 1928, he was dead.

Cecilia "Cissie" Haggerty with her three children
Margaret, Roland, and Norman, Tetagouche, NB,
before she returned to England in June 1928
(Photo courtesy of Charlene Skeels, great-granddaughter of Cecilia Haggerty)

Six months later, Cissie, and her three children returned to England on the Cunard ship RMS *Andania* by way of Montreal to Liverpool. Pat's oldest daughter, Lucy, was eleven years old in 1928, when Mrs. Haggerty and the children stayed at the Hennessy family homestead in Bathurst en route to England. Bea must have felt sorry for this poor Englishwoman, and allowed her to stay while arrangements were made for departure overseas. Lucy recalls that Mrs. Haggerty left some of her possessions behind, including a collection of colourful, glass peacock-shaped ornaments with real feathers that were hung on the Christmas tree for years. Where Cissie found the money to buy transatlantic tickets is unknown: as Augustine's wife, she should have been entitled to the proceeds from the sale of farm animals and equipment, but whether Augustine actually owned anything is debatable. It's unlikely her parents were able to help. When Cissie arrived back in

Manchester, she had to face the reality that there was no room for six people in her parents' two-bedroom house. Soon, the stock market crash of 1929 would be upon them, and as a single mother with few resources, Cissie made the difficult decision to put the children in St. Joseph's Catholic Orphanage in Salford, Manchester.

Cissie eventually found work at Clarks Atlas, an electrical manufacturing firm in Eccles, Manchester, where she was the secretary for many years. She saw the children on the weekends and they would come for visits, but they didn't live together again until 1936, when Cissie remarried. Her second husband, James Bird, was a ferryman who worked for the Manchester Ship Canal Company, which was established in 1885 to build the Manchester Ship Canal – a fifty-five-kilometre-long inland waterway linking Manchester with the Irish Sea that, in its day, was the world's longest river navigation canal. James rowed workers across the canal to their place of work. Cissie and James had a daughter, Sheila, born in 1939, and for the first time since leaving Canada in 1928, Cissie was surrounded by family again.

By the time Cissie remarried, Margaret was nearly fourteen years old, Roland was twelve, and Norman, the youngest, was dead, having contracted diphtheria at the orphanage. With a job, new husband, her two surviving children back in the fold, and a baby soon on the way, there was little time left for writing letters to Canada. Eight years after leaving Canada, the widow Cissie had started a new life.

But there might have been another reason to sever ties with her past in Canada. In April 1934, Cissie's brother-in-law, Thomas Haggerty, shot and killed his cousin Frank Haggerty in a fight over land in Tetagouche. At trial, Thomas was found guilty and sentenced to death, but his sentence was commuted to life in prison just two days before the execution was to take place. Thomas spent the rest of his life in prison. It was a sensational trial that was reported widely in the papers, and Cissie must have known about it. Interestingly, the last known correspondence from Cissie came in April 1934, the same month as the murder. In it was a studio photograph of Margaret, Norman, and Roland.

When Patrick went overseas, he tried to find Mrs. Haggerty in Manchester. Throughout his correspondence are references to his failed attempts to find the woman and her children. Letters he mailed to her last known address were returned, and his visits to Manchester came up empty handed: "Haven't found Mrs. Haggerty or at least Mrs. Bird but I am looking her up now. I expect word this week. If she is alive I can find her. Manchester was blitzed terrible. The police are looking her up." In August 1942, he wrote: "Manchester is a grand city with lots of scenery. I didn't see the Haggertys. I wonder if Mrs. Pat O'Kane hears from them yet." Pat never did find Mrs. Haggerty. After Margaret married James Skeels in 1942, Cissie, her husband James, and daughter Sheila moved to Liverpool Street, Eccles. Pat could have passed them on the street and not known it. As late as 1950, attempts were made through the Salvation Army to find Mrs. Haggerty/Mrs. Bird in Manchester, but to no avail.

In 2016, almost ninety years after Cissie left Canada, her descendants were traced to Manchester, where she had died in 1984 under the name Cecilia Bird. Her daughter Margaret and son Roland are gone now, too, and it seems they never spoke much about their Canadian experience. At five and four years old, they wouldn't have remembered much, but Margaret did say this about her father: "He was not a nice man." Still, Margaret never forgot her New Brunswick roots. In 1995, unbeknownst to the Hennessys, who had looked for her for so many years, she travelled from England with her eldest son to the family farm in Tetagouche, going back to reconnect with the place from which she, her mother, and brothers departed amid tragedy so long ago.

George Campbell of Fredericton served with 25 Company, No. 2 District, Canadian Forestry Corps, at Mar Lodge in the Cairngorms, where he played the bagpipes in the CFC band. Back row (left to right): Cecil Archibald, Charley Riley, unknown, George Campbell, David Bell; front row: Lou Ellis, Ken Alward. (Photo courtesy of George Campbell)

Chapter Six

Settling In for the Duration

Pat was happy in Scotland. For the first time in his life he had freedom, a little bit of money, and nobody telling him where to spend it. During the spring and early fall of 1941, he did some travelling, but when it started getting cold he was glad to have spent his money on a bedroll, rather than liquor, as had many others in camp: "We are having winter now. It is quite cold and wet. My bedroll comes in good just now. Everyone seems to be cold at night but I am glad I got it. For what I paid for it the rest bought beer and wine with their money."

Despite their remote location, the men could go to the YMCA Canteen and Recreation Room in Kiltarlity that had been established for the troops on August 15, 1941. There were at least two dances a week at Beauly, Kiltarlity, and Kirkhill, and popular films were screened on a regular basis in the camp's mess hall by the Canadian Legion Auxiliary Services. Travelling concert parties featuring Scottish musicians, comedians, and dancers also made the rounds of Highland logging camps. In January 1942, Pat wrote home about the Tartan Tonics Concert Party, held in 15 Company's mess hall. The Tartan Tonics were led by Scottish comedian Dave Bruce, whose troupe had just finished a three-week engagement at the Tivoli in Aberdeen. The CFC mess hall would have been a step down from the Tivoli, but the response from the soldiers was no less enthusiastic:

"We had a concert tonight. There were 10 people in the group. I served sandwiches after the show in the officers' mess. They were Scotch comedians, awful funny. Two twin sisters danced. Oh what tap dancers. They are about 17 year-old. We have a travelling show, about three a month during winter and long nights."

In late March 1942, almost twelve months since their arrival at Lovat No. 2, 15 Company reported that work had begun on construction of a recreation hut that would include a reading room and canteen facilities. The main hall would also include a stage and adequate dressing rooms and lighting to accommodate performers who were becoming part of the social life of the Canadians and their Scottish neighbours in the surrounding villages of Kiltarlity and Beauly. It was a sign that 15 Company was there to stay, and a nod to the importance of recreational facilities was that the unit designated £50 to interior furnishings. After the hall opened in May, visits from semi-professional and professional entertainers occurred more frequently, providing a welcome distraction and a morale booster to the troops. These ranged from the Canadian Forestry Corps Band, cobbled together from musicians in No. 2 District CFC, to the Seaforth Highlanders regimental band from Fort George, near Inverness, to performances by Canadian Army entertainment troupes the Kit Bags and Tin Hats. On May 11, 15 Company's war diary made note of the Kit Bags' arrival in camp: "The first concert in our new rec hall was put on by a Canadian Corps Concert Party 'The Kit Bags.' The show is the best we have seen here and was enthusiastically received by the whole COY." In September, it was the Tin Hats' turn to perform for the troops: "Tonight we enjoyed a very fine concert put on in our Recreation Hall by the Canadian 'Tin Hats' Concert Party. They are all artists and put across a really swell show." In September 1943, ENSA (the Entertainments National Service Association), the British organization charged with providing entertainment for those in uniform, put on a show at the recreation hall called "Stand by for Fun."

Monthly dances were also a regular fixture at the recreation hall. In late May 1943, a "Company Dance" featured an orchestra made up of musicians from 15 and 19 Companies. Whenever a dance was planned,

"Wren" Zoe (Blair) Boone worked as an airframe mechanic with the Fleet Air Arm. She was billeted at Novar House in Evanton when she was invited to a CFC dance at 15 Company's recreation hall.
(Melynda Jarratt Fonds, PANB)

local women were invited, and sometimes even the "Wrens" (members of the Women's Royal Naval Service, or WRNS) from Novar House in Evanton were brought in by lorry. Located twenty miles north of Beauly, near Novar House, Evanton was the site of a Royal Naval Air Station where Wrens like Zoe (Blair) Boone of Aberdeen worked in large hangars as checkers on Swordfish and Spitfire aircraft. Before Evanton, Boone was stationed at Machrihanish, on the west coast of Scotland, where she worked on modifying torpedo tubes for the Barracuda torpedo/dive bombers that attacked the German battleship *Tirpitz* on April 3, 1944. Boone later came to New Brunswick as war bride, settling in Rowena, near Plaster Rock. She remembers going to dances in Beauly and the No. 5 District CFC camps at Muir of Ord, Teanacoil, and Boblainy, where she met Pat Hennessy. "They would post a notice on the bulletin board in the dining room at Novar House and you had to put your name on it quick because there were only about 25 spaces in the lorry," she recalls. "Then they'd come

Beatrice with James and Roger in their RCAF great coats.
Roger is holding his daughter Patsy, born April 26, 1941.

get us at a certain time and we'd all pile in the back and make the long drive to the CFC camp. It was exciting and we girls were happy to meet Canadians because they were good dancers." Boone met Pat through one of the young Canadian soldiers who was a cookee. He invited her to the cook house, where Pat served them each a boiled egg. "I remember meeting him because eggs were rationed," she says. "It was the best egg I ever ate."

Although Pat seemed to enjoy the distraction that outside entertainment brought to the camp, it certainly wasn't his priority. In letters home, he talks about sitting alone in the little kitchen on payday and hearing the boys whooping it up in the recreation hall. Pat was more than thirty-five years older than the youngest CFC men and a complete teetotaller, and as a father and grandfather he had more important things on his mind. Every summer since they bought the farm with Bea's uncle Manus Kane, Pat had been home to help with the animals, bring in the harvest, and prepare the homestead for winter. The four sons, Roger, James, Bruno, and Bobby, and even nephew Tom could be relied on for farm work. At the peak of harvest season, Pat and Bea would bring in hired help. But life on the home front had changed dramatically since the war began, and with Pat's departure in December 1940, there was one less able-bodied man to do the heavy work. Still, the farm would have been manageable had Roger and James committed to staying in Bathurst. But, by summer 1941, everything Pat and Bea had worked so hard to build was in danger of collapsing when Roger joined the Royal Canadian Air Force (RCAF), leaving the burden of the farm work to James. Pat couldn't do much about Roger, who was now twenty-six, married, and the father of a baby girl, Mary Patricia Anne, known as "Patsy" (but whom Pat affectionately called "Paddy Ann"), but James was only nineteen, and Pat wrote frequently to Bea about keeping him in Bathurst. "James must stay with you," he says in a letter written on August 5, 1941. "No place for a boy here. Hell."

At camp that October, Pat met a young airman from Ottawa, and probably saw his own son in the fellow's demeanour. He insisted that Bea give Roger a special crucifix blessed by the Catholic archbishop of Westminster, Cardinal Hinsley. Hinsley was half-Irish and half-English and an outspoken critic of fascism even before the war. As one of the most senior representatives of the Catholic Church hierarchy in Britain, Hinsley was the next best thing to the pope as far as Pat was concerned. "I have a cross. One of Cardinal Hinsley's. A lady from Edinburgh gave me two. I will send it for Roger to wear. Tell him he must wear it at all times. I hope he will never have to come over here."

Roger enlisted in the air force in July 1941 with dreams of becoming a war artist. He was self-trained and had the natural talent to become a successful commercial artist. The RCAF sent Roger to the University of New Brunswick in Fredericton, and even though it meant there was one less man to work the farm, the family was supportive of his decision. News of Roger's enlistment got back to Lieutenant Bob Allen, Roger's friend in 15 Company. In a letter to his mother in Yarmouth, Nova Scotia, Allen asked her to write to Mrs. Hennessy and pass the following message on to Roger: "Tell Roger his father is fine and well-liked by all and also tell him to keep that hand in trim, for he should be able to use it in the line he is now taking." In November, Roger wrote to his mother asking for help assembling a portfolio of his work to submit for a job at the Scientific Research Labs in Ottawa. There was more than an urgency to his request; with the air battle in full swing over the skies of Britain, there was a very real possibility he would be sent overseas with the RCAF: "If you could gather a few of my drawings together and send them as soon as possible I will probably get it. Otherwise I will have to go air-crew. I gave Raymond Lavigne a picture once. I imagine if you explained to him what I want it for, you could get the lend of it and I will return it. Please hurry." In Toronto, Roger was interviewed by Flight Lieutenant Bishop, an Englishman who happened to be a professional draftsman. The interview lasted the whole afternoon, and Roger said Bishop must have asked him "a thousand questions to find out what I know so he could place me." Roger told Bishop of his desire to become a war artist, but Roger's lack of a formal art school education put him at a disadvantage. Instead of war artist, Bishop said Roger should become a draftsman. His hopes dashed, Roger tried to put the situation into perspective: "In the end he said I would be a lot more valuable as a draftsman than artist, as there were two fellows at the same time, one who had passed through the BC School of Art and the other the Toronto Art School. This last fellow exhibited in the Exhibition. He is going to send me to Hamilton, Ontario as soon as there is a vacancy. I will take a structural drafting course." Ironically, Roger created the cover artwork for Father Hickey's *The Scarlet Dawn*. Although denied his chance to be a war artist, Roger's painting of the North Shore Regiment facing the high cement wall at St-Aubin-sur-Mer on D-Day is one of the most recognizable works of art depicting New Brunswickers in the Second World War.

That left James, who graduated from high school the summer of 1941 and was working at Bathurst Power and Paper. In a long letter to James written before Christmas 1941, Pat asks about the farm, and makes it clear that the boy must stay with his mother in order to keep operations going: "James how is hay selling now and did you sell all you had this spring? Has Uncle Alex the horses this winter? How many cattle are you keeping this winter? How is the old barn? Did you get it fixed up for the winter? I suppose it will be quite cold. James how are the boys getting on at school? How is Mamma? I want you to stay with her until I get home again. With

Bobby, Beatrice, and Bruno outside the family homestead in Bathurst. By 1944, all of the Hennessy males were in the military, including fourteen-year-old Bobby, who was in the air cadets, and Bruno who had joined the army.

a job at the mill you can help so much at home, for your mother needs you." But James had no intention of staying in Bathurst while there was a war going on. In January 1942, he sold his Harley-Davidson motorcycle to a neighbour for $100, to be paid in four instalments of $25, and, over Pat's fierce objections, enlisted in the air force. With the backlog in mail delivery, however, Pat didn't find out about it for three months. And that wasn't the only thing James did: in February 1943, he got married in Montreal to Frances Garrett, a Bathurst woman who was working in a munitions factory. By early 1944, James was in Britain with the RCAF.

Then Bruno, young and cocky at age sixteen, tried to enlist. He was furious when the recruiting officer told him to "come back for the next war, sonny," but he didn't have to wait long: by 1944, Bruno was in the army, too.

The last son left was Bobby. After Roger and then James joined up, Bobby and Bruno took over the farm with their mother and some hired help, but it was never the same. When he was thirteen, Bobby joined the

After their first meeting in Bathurst in August 1940, Norwegian merchant mariner Henrik Wesenberg and Pat's youngest daughter Anna saw each other only four times during the war. By June 1946, they were married and on their way to Norway, where they lived for eight years before returning to Canada. In this photo taken at the Bathurst train station, Lucy, Sidney Jarratt, Anna, Henrik, and Roger's wife, Eileen, pose for the camera near the big "Bathurst" sign before Henrik leaves to return to his ship, the SS *Bergholm*, in Halifax.

air cadets, which took him away from the farm when he was most needed. All five males in the Hennessy family were in the military now.

Pat's daughters, Lucy and Anna, helped with domestic chores, but they couldn't do the heavy lifting required to run a farm. Nor did they want to: they had their distinctly women's sphere and the men had theirs. Pat didn't want his daughters joining the military, either. When he heard from Lucy that Anna was thinking of joining the women's services, he shot off a letter to Bea: "Don't let her join. It is no place for a girl. You will need her at home." Lucy worked briefly at Bathurst Power and Paper when the war broke out, but it wasn't the kind of work she was used to, so she returned to Dr. Densmore's office as his medical secretary. Besides, she was engaged to be married in August 1942 to Sidney Jarratt.

Sidney's father was a papermaker who had emigrated to Canada from England at the turn of the century. He had been the superintendent of Bathurst Power and Paper, a powerful position in the community, but he died suddenly in 1930. His American-born wife Glenys could have returned to her native New Hampshire, but she decided to stay in Bathurst, where their two boys had grown up. Sidney was sent to the private Rothesay Collegiate School, and graduated in 1933 at the height of the Depression. Through family connections, he was hired as a lab technician at the paper mill, while his younger brother William stayed at home and attended public school in Bathurst. The Jarratts were Anglican, and in those days marriage between two faiths was frowned upon. To appease Lucy and her family, Sidney converted to Catholicism. Aware as any young man would have been of the social importance of joining the military, he tried to enlist with the North Shore Regiment at the armoury in Bathurst, but was rejected on medical grounds. Sidney's brother William, however, had joined the air force, and was now Flight Lieutenant Jarratt, stationed overseas with the RCAF. Sidney didn't want to be the only man left behind, so he went up to Campbellton to try his luck with the recruiting office there. But try as he might, he couldn't get past the medical, so to his great regret he ended up working at the mill, becoming the only man connected to the Hennessy family who didn't serve in the military during the war.

Anna was still at the Company's Woodlands Division, but in August 1940, she met Henrik Wesenberg, a young sea captain from Oslo, Norway. Henrik was at sea aboard the SS *Bergholm* when the Germans invaded Norway in April 1940. To prevent its merchant marine from falling into enemy hands, Norway's King Haakon VII sent out a call over the radio instructing all ships to head for the nearest friendly port. It was a wise move that kept two-thirds of the country's shipping intact and made Norway the only government-in-exile that was able to pay its own way during the Second World War. Henrik's ship went to Lunenburg, Nova Scotia, where it became part of the Norwegian government-in-exile's maritime fleet.

Henrik and Anna met when the *Bergholm* made its one and only trip to Bathurst Harbour to pick up a load of lumber in August 1940. Henrik fell and broke his arm, and had the limb set by Dr. Densmore in Bathurst. While waiting in the office for the plaster cast to set, Henrik struck up a conversation with Lucy and asked her to go out to a movie. Lucy declined the offer, saying she was already engaged to be married, but that her sister Anna might go out on a double date. At first Anna refused: "There was no way she was going to go out with a foreigner," said Lucy. But after some arm twisting, Lucy, Sidney, Anna, and Henrik went out together to see the movie *South of the Border*, starring Gene Autry. Wearing an officer's white uniform with a cape swung over his shoulder, the handsome Norwegian quite literally swept Anna, and the rest of the family, off their feet. In May 1940, Henrik helped evacuate British soldiers from Dunkirk, and went on to do convoy duty on the Atlantic and at Scapa Flow, the British naval base in the Orkney Islands. He received a commendation for bravery while under German air attack on the English Channel, and he personally disarmed a German officer, taking the man's Luger pistol as a souvenir. Henrik survived to tell the tale, and in 1946 he returned to marry Anna and take her home to Norway. There, she became a "Bride of the Midnight Sun," as the press called Canadian women who married Norwegians during the war.

But all that was in the distant future. In August 1941, Pat's concerns had more to do with the state of the farm than with the increasingly complicated lives of his adult children, who, it seemed, were leaving the family farm behind. By this time, Pat had been gone from Bathurst for nine months, the longest he had been away from home even when he was working in the woods. Frustrated with the lack of information, he took to writing his teenage son Bruno, the most unreliable of all his children, to find out what was going on with the farm: "Bruno did you get a letter with a picture of a boat I sent it to Momma? Let me know if you got it. How is the cows? Is the Heifer milking. How is she? Is she cross to milk? Where have you the calves this summer? How many chickens have you this summer? Bruno send me all the news." Similar questions were asked of Bea in another letter, along with instructions on how to cover up the old well to prevent Bobby and young Tommy Moran from falling through. Sitting in his room at night, wondering what was going on in Bathurst, Pat must have been very worried about that old well because he even included a drawing that showed how to cover it up. "I think you should have a new plank top on the old well. Do it right away and put a fence around it to keep the boys off it."

As fall weather descended upon the Highlands, Pat didn't get out of camp much, not even to visit his new friends Don and Hannah Fraser at Old Downie or John Lee and Alice at Bonnyview. What a contrast it must have been from the summer, when the sun barely touched the horizon before 10 p.m. and was up again over the hills at 4 a.m. Now, those long, warm days were over, and winter lay ahead. In the privacy of his living quarters, Pat had plenty of time to think about what was happening in Bathurst and to ask, once again, the questions that still had not been answered: "Well we haven't got any mail for some time. The last letter I got from Lucy was No 10. There was a lot lost not long ago and I suppose mine was with the missing. The only thing is to keep writing. . . . I sent you a picture of the highland hills and heather from Inverness. Let me know if you get it. . . . Say how is the potatoes and the oats this fall? How is the apples? We never see one over here at all."

In early December, Pat went on leave to Stirling. In a letter to Bea, he marvels that he was at the very place where so many famous battles had taken place, yet the Scots think nothing of it: "I was through the Castle and I saw where the Battle at Stirling Bridge was fought. Also Bannockburn. All those places are marked now. It is marvelous to see. I was to the very balcony where Mary Queen of Scots walked and sat and viewed the countryside and the city. You know it gives one the chills when you think of it. I often say if you could only see it. No one thinks any thing about it here, even the children never go to see it. They say, 'Oh that's nothing. Only a wee battle' or say "I no go thair'." While Pat was at Stirling, the saloon at D.R. MacKenzie's in Kiltarlity was proclaimed "Out of Bounds" to all ranks before 5 p.m. during the week and 1 p.m. on Saturday. What led to the prohibition is unknown, but it might have been a preventive measure in advance of the inevitable Christmas drinking that was sure to take place on the first holiday away from Canada. On the morning of December 21, Pat and twenty-five other Roman Catholics in the company set off by truck to have Confession and Mass at St. Mary's, Beauly. For Pat, it was important to get to church for Christmas, since there would be no midnight Mass due to the blackout.

The unit was also about to celebrate its first Christmas in Scotland with a special dinner for the men served by the officers and sergeants. Pat expected to be busy for the next four days, and he hoped the meal would be a success. He need not have worried: with a menu that included a pint of beer, roast turkey, roast pork, dressing, potatoes, carrots, turnips, Brussels sprouts, bread plum pudding, and coffee, everyone had their fill. In fact, it was noted in the war diary that the cookhouse staff did an excellent job: "dinner was appetizing enough to tickle the palate of the most discriminating gourmet."

While Pat was toiling away in the kitchen preparing turkeys for Christmas dinner, two non-commissioned officers who were lucky enough to get nine days' leave headed out of camp on the 22nd. In the war diary, this humorous description gives a sense of the camaraderie between the men on their first Christmas away from home: "Sgts. Luford and Mersereau started today on leave to visit friends in the south for Christmas. Both these men are Veterans, affable, reliable and with a ready store of native wit and are very popular with everyone in the Company. As I saw them stroll out of camp with their complete equipment plus a goose, bog cranberries and other fixings for their goose, and of course, the inevitable quart of gin, I couldn't help but remarking every unit should have its old Bill, but we have two in ours."

That Christmas Eve, the weather turned mild, and Pat didn't feel like celebrating. While the other men were "feeling jolly" after a few drinks at the canteen, Pat retreated to his kitchen in the officers' mess and wrote a letter to Bea about the invitation he and the other Roman Catholics in 15 Company had received to attend morning Mass at Beaufort Castle: "This is Xmas Eve. It is just as mild as June tonight. It does not seem like Xmas. We never had any frost yet. The wind was cold, that's all. The boys are feeling jolly. They are at the canteen. It is now 10 o'clock p.m. It has been dark since five p.m. We got the turkeys all ready for dinner tomorrow. We have no midnight mass on account of black out but Father Geddes is having mass at Beaufort Castle. We will be there although we have a terrible long way to go. The mass is at 8:30 a.m."

The Lovats' friendly invitation to the Roman Catholics in 15 Company is just one example of how the Scots went out of their way to forge relations with the Canadians during the war. Every year while the Canadians were stationed at the Lovat Estate, men from No. 5 District were invited to Christmas Mass at Beaufort Castle, and Pat went to every one. There is no record, however, of the Canadians' visits to Beaufort Castle in the war diaries of 15 Company or No. 5 District Headquarters. Archival records from Beaufort Castle are not available, but it is likely that official invitations from Lord and Lady Lovat would have come through No. 5 District Headquarters, then down the line to 15 Company's commanding officer, who, in turn, would have selected the most pious of the Catholic soldiers in its ranks to represent the company. Pat was left star-struck by his hosts and the opulent interior of the grand Scottish castle, with it two giant ballrooms and own private chapel. In a letter to Bea following the Christmas morning Mass, Pat wrote: "This invitation we got to the castle is something rare. It was wonderful to see the lovely chapel in the castle and some lovely statues of the Blessed Virgin and the Crucifix and Joseph. A very magnificent altar.... So Bee when you look at Beaufort Castle think I was at mass on Christmas morning December 25, 1941. So wishing you a Happy New Year, Pat. Answer soon."

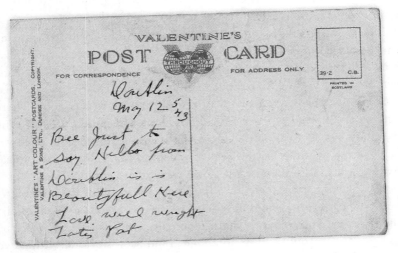

A postcard from Pat in Dublin. On the back it reads, "May 12, 1943.
Bee, Just to say Hello from Dublin. It is beautiful here.
Love Lots. Will write. Pat."

Chapter Seven

Ireland

Pat had barely arrived in Scotland when he started talking about plans to visit Ireland. To Pat, there was no difference between Northern Ireland and the republic to the south. The political distinctions that divided the two countries meant little to a man for whom visiting his ancestral homeland would be the culmination of a lifelong dream. The problem, however, was that the Irish government had elected to stay neutral with respect to the war — or "the Emergency," as it was officially called in the south. Although it was perfectly acceptable to visit Northern Ireland, which was part of the United Kingdom, the south's neutrality meant that it was both illegal and risky for servicemen of either the Allied or Axis forces to be caught in uniform on its soil. That quickly became evident to the hundreds of airmen whose planes crashed or force landed in Ireland during the war: according to the Curragh.info website, more than 167 planes went down between 1939 and 1945, and the surviving British, American, Canadian, and German crews were held as prisoners-of-war (POWs) in the K-Lines Internment Camp at Curragh Army Barracks in Dublin.

The K-Lines was a POW camp like no other: both British and German prisoners were permitted to wear civilian clothes in public and had access to recreation facilities and wireless radio. They were allowed to attend religious services and even had vegetable gardens. British prisoners were given passes to visit their wives who travelled to northern Ireland, and there was a limited parole system for both British and German POWs. Over time, parole was expanded to include permission to attend dances, the theatre, and horse races, as well as visit hotels and even private homes, so long as the POW signed a document promising on his honour to return at night: "I hereby promise to be back in the compound at ____ o'clock and, during my absence, not to take part in any activity connected with the war or prejudicial to the interests of the Irish state."

Despite the relaxed camp environment, escape from K-Lines was officially prohibited. German prisoners would have had considerable difficulty making their getaway, as the nearest German-occupied country was France, but British soldiers could count on assistance getting across the nearby border to Northern Ireland through the "Escape Club," formed by pro-British Irish civilians.

As Allies, Canadians were welcome in Northern Ireland, and many did make the journey, using it as a stepping-off point to cross the border into the south. The only requirements were that they wear civilian clothes and have a relative to visit. Whether Pat knew exactly where his people had come from in Ireland is doubtful. It was nearly two hundred years since his ancestor, Edward Hennessy, had left for Canada, and Pat had no known relatives to call upon — even the knowledge of the specific county or parish Edward came from had long been lost to memory. Still, Pat was determined to fulfill his dream of a pilgrimage to Ireland now that he was so close. But first, he had to apply for permission from his commanding officer, and, in addition to the clothing problem, he had to locate the missing relatives.

Father Hickey, the padre of the North Shore Regiment and a friend of Pat's from Bathurst, faced the same problem about non-existent Irish relatives. The priest's trips to Ireland feature prominently in his book *The Scarlet Dawn*, so perhaps he had some advice for Pat. In this excerpt from his book, Father Hickey explains how he managed to find a way around the military bureaucracy to visit the Emerald Isle:

As Ireland was a neutral country, you could get there only on certain conditions: You had to have close relatives there, and of course, you couldn't go dressed in Khaki. Mother, God bless her, solved the second problem by sending over my black suit; and between Colonel Buell and me, we solved the first. I went into the Colonel's office, clicked my heels, saluted, and like a condemned man making one last request, I begged for permission to visit my Uncle Pat in County Cork one more time before I'd die. The Colonel was just new to the regiment, and fearful no doubt, that the curse of Cromwell would fall upon him, without a question, but with that well-known smile and a quick glance at me, he signed. But now, I'm sure that in his lifetime the good Colonel must have put his name to things with less probability of truth in them than my passport, for surely it wouldn't be hard for him to imagine that there must be a Pat Hickey roaming around somewhere in County Cork: and if his conscience still bothers him I'll tell him that, in another unit, a fellow I knew got to Ireland to visit a relative called Mr. O'Gresham: now Gresham, if you want to know, is nothing more than the name of a swanky hotel in Dublin. Another lad too, with such an un-Hibernian name as Kurst, took a longing for the auld sod, and when asked his reason, replied that he wanted to visit the O'Kurses.

Even if Pat had obtained permission to travel, no CFC man was going very far from Scotland in spring 1941: with the Battle of Britain raging overhead, England was off limits. So, too, was Northern Ireland after Luftwaffe bombing raids on Belfast in March and April 1941 that killed 1,100 people. "We can't go to Ireland or England now. Too much bombing," he told Anna on May 12. That summer and fall, thoughts of Ireland were never far from Pat's mind. On August 12, he told Bea that his request to travel was granted. Again in September and November, his letters talk about plans to visit Ireland, but new prohibitions on travel put a stop to that. In January 1942, Pat wrote with news that he was going to Ireland on his next leave with a cook named Burt Burk, whose parents lived there. Burk was an Irish-American who had made his way to Canada to enlist in Nova Scotia-based 13 Company. He arrived in Scotland with a group of five CFC companies in July 1941, and was serving with 13 Company in Southesk, Brechin, a small village southwest of Aberdeen. Burk and Pat probably met at basic training at Valcartier, where 13 and 15 Companies were billeted close together — or perhaps they were introduced to each other through a Forestry Corps member in Scotland who knew about Pat's desire to see Ireland. "He is a real nice young man," Pat wrote Bea. "He has been to see [his parents] on his landing leave. He writes me often."

Their plans must have fallen through, however, because another eight months passed before Pat finally travelled to Ballymena, Northern Ireland, in late August 1942. Father Joseph Austin McGuire, the Roman Catholic padre of the CFC, had been urging Pat to visit Ireland for some time, so Pat likely gave up on Burk and decided to go on his own: "Father McGuire is here to have mass tomorrow. He is a tall, blond man, very nice. He has been to Ireland and he told me I must go to see St. Patrick's Temple. Then, he said, one is ready for Heaven. It is marvellous." From August 28 to September 4, Pat roamed the cities and countryside of Northern Ireland, even befriending a Catholic family, the Targetts, who invited him for dinner. It was the fulfillment of a dream for this fourth-generation Irish-Canadian, who became the first member of his family in two centuries to visit the Old Country. He wrote glowingly of the people he met and the places he saw, which seemed to live up to every one of his expectations: "I just wish you could see the place," he writes to Bea after returning from Ireland in September. "Every one says that Ireland is the prettiest place on this side of the Atlantic and what I saw it is right. It is more beautiful than England or Scotland." Pat is amazed to see palm trees "just like in Florida." He speaks of the women going about "with shawls over their heads" and "donkeys hauling peat for fuel." He notes the fields "are so green and all fenced off with hedges and the people are awful clever." "They used me awful good when I was there," he writes. "They would say 'Pat Hennessy! All the way from Canada! Come in and have some tea'."

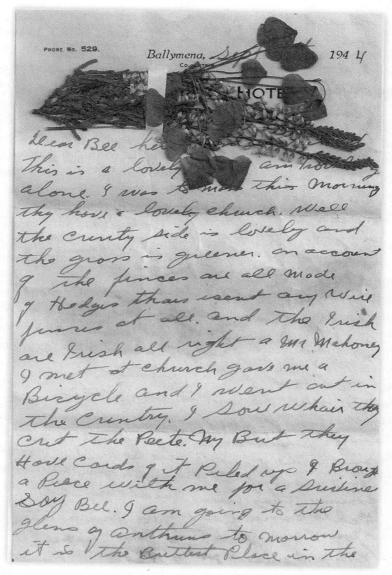

PHONE NO. 529.   Ballymena, ____ 194 4
CO. ANTRIM

____ HOTE____

Dear Bee here ____ ____ ____
This is a lovely ____ am ____
alone. I was to ____ this morning
they have a lovely church. Well
the country side is lovely and
the grass is greener. on account
of the fences are all made
of Hedges there isent any wire
fences at all. and the Irish
are Irish all right a Mr Mahoney
I met at church gave me a
Bicycle and I went out in
the Country. I saw where they
cut the Peete. My But they
Have Cords of it Piled up I Broug
a Piece with me for a Suitine
Say Bee. I am going to the
glens of anthrum to morrow
it is the Beutest Place in the

In September 1944, Pat went on his third trip to Ireland.
In his letters from Scotland, he would attach slips of heather;
here, he includes shamrocks as a reminder of his Irish travels.

He describes a trip to an ancient site where it was believed no less than Saint Patrick himself once walked the ground: "I went out about eight miles on the Ballymena Road and on the hillside is marked where Saint Patrick herded sheep when he was a slave. I was taken to the very spot by a very old man and he said this is the very rock he used to sit on. It is marked. God bless him." Ever mindful of the importance of Saint Patrick's Day, Pat promises to send some shamrocks to Bathurst: "I brought a root of shamrock with me. It is growing good. I shall send you a bunch for 17 March." "Just close your eyes and imagine," he writes in another letter to his daughter Anna. "It is more beautiful than one can ever dream of. I am going again someday."

That "someday" came again in May 1943, when Pat was granted a second privileged leave to travel to Northern Ireland. From letters he wrote during that trip, we know he crossed the border into the south and spent time in Dublin, where he stayed at O'Neill's Hotel and Restaurant on Gardiner Street, near Nelson's Pillar, touring around the city and even visiting the Dublin Zoo. Two official travel documents from that trip survive. The first is an army embarkation card dated May 8, 1943, for the port of Stranraer, on the North Channel between Scotland and Ireland; the second is an army "Permission to Travel" form, and in it is a clue about how Pat managed to travel to a country in which he had no known relatives. Under the column "Name and Address of Relative" appears the name "Miss Bella Leach of Ballemena [sic], Northern Ireland"—an aunt whom Pat is supposedly visiting. As there was no known Hennessy relative in the whole of Ireland, and certainly not an aunt by the name of Bella Leach, one can come to no other conclusion than that Pat—like Father Hickey—lied on his application form, drawing into question the "thorough reliability" to which his commanding officer so willingly vouched!

May 8, 1943

To Whom It May Concern
Travel to: (Northern Ireland)

The thorough reliability of the under mentioned soldier of the Canadian Forestry Corps, having been vouched for by the O.C. of his unit, his application for leave is approved and authority for him to travel to the above mentioned country is hereby authorized.

Captain and Adjutant J.J. Scanlon, for Commander, Canadian Forestry Corps

In early September 1944, Pat made a third trip to Northern Ireland. He seemed surprised that so few of the Forestry Corps men showed any interest in visiting Northern Ireland when he and Father McGuire couldn't seem to get enough of the country: "I am the only one from our COY to come except the padre. He just loves it here in Ballymena. The stores are nice and well kept. But one can't buy anything without coupons. In the south you can buy anything." Rationing in Northern Ireland meant that even a postcard was difficult to get: a card Pat bought at the Grand Central Hotel in Belfast doesn't even have a picture on the front! "This is all I have to send. One can't get anything without coupons [and] we haven't got any."

Pat adored the people who were so welcoming to a friendly Canadian soldier with an Irish name like Hennessy: "This morning at church you could think they knew me all my life. Hello Canada! Are you Irish? Then you can guess the rest." A Mr. Mahoney, whom he met at church, even loaned him a bike, and he pedalled out to a place where peat was cut, getting a piece for a souvenir. He was in awe of the greenery, and said he'd heard plenty of fairy stories during his visits there. A day trip to the Glens of Antrim was one of the highlights of his visit. "It is the prettiest place in the north," he says to Bea, "The only thing I wish you were here to see it all."

HEAD QUARTERS, CANADIAN FORESTRY CORPS
Canadian Army Overseas

.....8th May,.........1943

TO WHOM IT MAY CONCERN:

LEAVE TO: (NORTHERN IRELAND)
xxxxxx

The thorough reliability of the undermentioned soldier of the Canadian Forestry Corps, having been vouched for by the O/C. of his Unit, his application for leave is approved and authority for him to travel to the above mentioned country is hereby authorized:—

NAME OF SOLDIER   NAME AND ADDRESS OF RELATIVE

G.48191,   Miss. Bella Leach, (Aunt)
Pte. Hennessy, P.J.   Bellamena,
No. 15 Coy.,   Northern Ireland.
Canadian Forestry Corps.

(This is the above mentioned's second visit to Northern Ireland.)

Corps H.Q. Canadian Forestry
Corps, C.A.S.F.
APPROVED
MAY 8 1943

Office Commanding, C.F.C.

(J.J. Scanlon) Captain & Adjutant
for Commander,
Canadian Forestry Corps

Canadian servicemen could only travel to Northern Ireland if they had a relative there. Many got around the prohibition by making up a name. In this document asking permission to travel, Pat claims to be visiting his "aunt," Bella Leach.

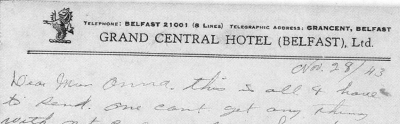

TELEPHONE: BELFAST 21001 (8 LINES) TELEGRAPHIC ADDRESS: GRANCENT, BELFAST
GRAND CENTRAL HOTEL (BELFAST), Ltd.

Nov. 28/43

Dear Mrs Onna. this is all I have to send. one cant get anything with out copons. so we havent got any. so Happy be you new year and Xmas. Hope Santy will be good to yous how are the Boys. with Love to all

P JH

A postcard without a picture: rationing in Northern Ireland

By Christmas 1944, Pat's time in Britain was coming to an end, and he hoped to make the most of what little time he had left by taking one more trip to Ireland. In the previous twelve months, he had had only two privileged leaves of seven days each, one in January and the other in June. He was now entitled to nine days' leave, but due to the fighting on the continent, he was asked to postpone it until after the holidays. That Christmas, he made one last turkey dinner with all the fixings for the officers. After his duties were over on December 30, he spent the evening with the Chisholms at Femnock. On New Year's Day 1945, he wrote to Anna with news that he was making a final trip to Ireland: "My next letter to you will be from Ireland. I am bound for the Shannon River. Look on the map and you can imagine I am in Ireland."

When Pat returned to Canada in September 1945, he told his family that he had borrowed the "Padre's" suit when he went to Ireland. Pat's children always assumed the "Padre" was Father Hickey, but it could just as easily have been Father McGuire of the CFC. A hint can be found in Father Hickey's memoir *The Scarlet Dawn*, in which the priest speaks about the suit his mother sent him and how useful it was — not only for him, but also for all the other Canadian padres who needed civilian clothes for their Irish travels. Pat knew Father Hickey well, and it's not much of a stretch to believe that he, too, wore Father Hickey's suit in Ireland.

How many times did I go to Ireland? Father Hickey asks.... Well, it's a funny thing about that. My pants were there six times; my coat four times; my shoes five, but I myself only three. You see, it was this way: I had the only black suit among the chaplains, so it soon became sort of a family possession. My pants travelled back and forth to Ireland until the big Rev. Angus Kerr left the nether end of them on a wire fence somewhere in County Kerry. My nice pair of shoes made the rounds of Ireland several times, until Father McCarney, in a moment of Celtic enthusiasm, stuck his feet too close to a turf fire in a cottage somewhere in Connemara and burnt the two soles right off them. Bad enough at that, but before he returned them, he had them repaired by an army cobbler. After that they looked about as neat as a pair of Dutchman's wooden clogs. My hat? Oh that only when I went, because ne'er a one of them had head enough to fill it.

I still have the remains of that old black suit and what is left of my fine pair of Hartt shoes. And when I get longing for Ireland, which is often, I just look at those time-worn trousers and I see the wire fences in County Kerry. I look at that pair of twisted shoes with their rugged soles, and I smell the peat in the bogs and see a turf fire, in a cozy cottage along the rugged coast of Connemara.

Chapter Eight

Social Relations

Dominion Day in Scotland as celebrated by the Canadians will
not soon be forgotten by local residents in Beauly and area.
Starting with a sports program which lasted nearly all day and
ending with a dance in the town hall in Beauly. . . . Scotland saw
for the first time possibly the art of log hurling, sawing contest,
chopping and other typical Canadian lumbering sports. In addi-
tion there were races, ball games and soccer etc. Local opinion is
that these Canadians play hard and work hard.

—15 Company War Diary, July 7, 1941

On July 1, 1941, 15 and 18 Companies and No. 5 District Headquarters held a sports day to mark Canada's Dominion Day "in a manner befitting the occasion." Pat kept a copy of the Dominion Day program and sent it along to Bea, who faithfully glued it into her growing scrapbook. According to the itinerary, soccer, baseball, and track and field events were held at the soccer field in Kiltarlity village, and "lumbering sports" took place at the log pond at the newly built Kiltarlity mill. Judges for the track and field events were Major Williams, Lieutenants Allen and Perry, and Company Sergeant Major Mott. An evening dance took place at Phipps Hall, which was built in 1903 by Henry Phipps Jr., a lifelong friend and business partner of Scottish-American philanthropist Andrew Carnegie.

The all-day event was open to all ranks and civilians, and it did not go unnoticed by locals, especially the children, whose quiet little Highland village had recently been invaded by Canadian foresters with huge trucks, tools, and equipment they had never seen before. Indeed, the children were positively thrilled by the arrival of the Canadians and their sweets, chocolate, and all kinds of goodies that were rationed in Scotland during

DOMINION DAY

1 July, 1941.

Programme

Place.	Sports	Soccer Field, Kiltarlity Village Log Pond, Kiltarlity Mill.
	Dance.	Phipp's Hall, Beauly.
Time	Sports.	1000 hours and 1330 hours Softball finals @ 1900 hours
	Dance & Presentation of prizes	2100 hours and 2200 hours.
Entries	All Events	Must be in the respective Orderly Rooms by 1200 hours 30-6-41. These entries will be picked up by Mr. Jas. Bell, Y.M.C.A. representative at this hour.
Policing.	At Dance.	In charge of 1 N.C.O. and 1 O/R from Nos. 15 & 18 Coy. and H.Q. Each detail to look after their own men.
Admission	Sports & Dance.	Free to all ranks and civilians.

```
XXXXXXXXXXXXXXXXXXXXXXXXXXXXX
     XXXXXXXXXXXXXXXXX
        XXXXXXXXX
         XXXXX
           X
```

A meeting was held at 2000 hours at Corps Headquarters with representatives of H.Q., # 15 Coy. and No. 18 Coy. present. The draw for the games was made with the results as shown below. Judges for the different events were appointed. Owing to the shortage of time available it is not possible to advise the different judges personally, but it is hoped that they will co-operate with the committee and be on hand at the appointed time to carry out their duties. Where starters are needed the judges will pick a starter from the personnel present on the grounds. The schedule of events decided on is as follows:-

Morning.

| 1000 hours. | Soccer game H.Q. vs. No. 18 Coy.
Time of game: 30 min. each half. |
| 1100 hours. | Softball game H.Q. vs. No. 15 Coy.
7 innings. |

1000 hours	Event.	Judge.
	Broad Jump	Lt. Perry
	Hop-step-& jump	Lt. Allen
	Shot Put	Major Williams
	Throwing Softball	C.S.M. Mott

Note: Each contestant to have three tries - best to count.

Schedule of the CFC's events, Dominion Day, 1941. In addition to softball, soccer, and athletics, sports included log rolling and log cutting. The celebrations concluded with a public dance at Phipps Hall in Beauly.

Dances at Phipps Hall led to many romances between local women and the Canadian foresters, including Charlie Gunning and Dolly Connell, who married and moved to New Brunswick after the war.

the war. Even the *Inverness Courier* made note of the Canadian celebrations: "On July 1, 1941 there was a Canadian Lumberman's Sports Day and Dance held locally. The sports were actually held in the Parish of Kiltarlity, but the Dance was at Phipps Hall." This would be the first of many dances and concert parties held at Phipps Hall and later at 15 Company's own recreation hall, which was officially opened in May 1942.

It was at CFC dances like these all over Scotland that local women had a chance to meet an array of eligible, mostly young Canadians, and love often blossomed. One of the first romances to take root in 15 Company was between a nineteen-year-old Kiltarlity woman, Dolina "Dolly" Connell, and twenty-eight-year-old Charlie Gunning of Lower Gagetown, New Brunswick. Dolly met Charlie at a concert in Kiltarlity soon after 15 Company arrived in April 1941. Charlie, originally from Ayr, Scotland, had emigrated to Lower Gagetown when he was just fifteen as one of the "Cossar Boys," a Scottish child migration scheme so named after their benefactor, Dr. George Cossar. Cossar came from a wealthy Glasgow family, and was sensitized to the plight of homeless men during

Training farm for Scottish boys, Lower Gagetown, NB, established by
Dr. George Cossar of Glasgow. The "Cossar Boys" learned how to work
a farm; many stayed on in the province. (New Brunswick Museum 1989.95.14)

his student days at Rugby School and Oxford. He established soup kitchens
and shelters in Glasgow, but is best known for organizing a movement
of young Scottish boys to work on farms in New Brunswick, starting in
1910. Cossar purchased a farm and apple orchard in Lower Gagetown that
provided jobs and training in modern agricultural methods to otherwise
unemployed or orphaned Scottish boys. Of the one thousand children
Cossar recruited to Canada, more than seven hundred remained in the
province, among them Charlie Gunning.

Although the Cossar Boys experiment had its detractors, Charlie was
one of the lucky child migrants who loved the Cossar farm. Even after
he left Lower Gagetown to work in a logging camp up the Saint John
River near Hartland, Charlie remained friends with the caretakers, Mr.
and Mrs. John Jackson, who treated him like a son. In Hartland, Charlie
befriended William and Ivey Fraser, a Scottish couple who had come to

New Brunswick from Kiltarlity. The Frasers ran the post office in Hartland, and Charlie met them when he went in one day to buy a stamp. After he joined 15 Company in 1940, they gave him the address of Ivey's sister, Jeannie MacKintosh, who lived in Kiltarlity with her husband and young children. The Frasers told Charlie to look the family up when he went to Scotland. Little did they know that 15 Company would end up in Boblainy Forest, quite literally on the MacKintoshes' doorstep.

Dolly Connell, born in Glasgow in 1922, was the youngest of four children. After her father and mother died of tuberculosis, six-year-old Dolly, her two sisters Lillian and Betty, and brother Ian were sent to live with their elderly grandparents in the Highlands at Glenfinnan, west of Fort William. It was a long walk to school from their grandparents' home, and the children frequently missed classes. Lillian had contracted TB from their mother and was sick often, eventually dying of the disease. Teachers' complaints about their poor school attendance brought the family to the attention of social services, and the three youngest were removed from their grandparents' care and sent to live with Hugh and Jessie Fraser, their new foster parents, near Kiltarlity. Hugh and Jessie were the brother and sister of the famed Willie "The Moon" Fraser, to whom Lord Lovat dedicated the first chapter of his memoir, *March Past*. Like Willie, Hugh and Jessie also worked at the Lovat Estate, but they didn't live at Old Downie; rather, they kept up the family croft at Achnacloich, near Boblainy Wood, next door to the MacKintosh family. The croft at Achnacloich was one of hundreds on vast stretches of land owned by Lord Lovat. According to Scottish tradition, tenants paid rent to the landowner and were allowed to make a living raising crops and farm animals. The Frasers' croft had passed down the male line from their grandfather to their father and then to Hugh. Unmarried, Hugh and Jessie were the last of eleven siblings to live there.

At the time, it was common practice for Highland families to take in orphans from rural areas and cities like Glasgow and Edinburgh. In the 1920s, '30s, and '40s, hundreds of foster children were brought in from Glasgow, and social workers were eager to place them in homes. In her memoir, *Past Forgetting*, Veronica Maclean, Lord Lovat's sister, wrote of her mother Lady Laura's social "crusades" with the "Glasgow Orphans":

The "Orphans"...were farmed out in those days to foster parents all over the Highlands. There was nothing intrinsically wrong with that..., and the poor children almost certainly enjoyed happier lives than they would have had in institutions in the heart of Glasgow city. Those who landed with good families and motherly women were often brought up as real members of the family, and even if they did provide cheap labour and seven shillings [35 pence] a head a week for their keep, they also received some of the affection and all the chances in life of their foster brethren.

Hugh and Jessie were just one of many foster parents in the area, and it was the Connell children's good luck that they were distantly related. "Uncle Hugh" and "Aunt Jessie," as Dolly called them, loved the three children, and even defied social workers' orders by taking their charges to Inverness by train to meet their elderly grandmother. Dolly grew up at Achnacloich, and was seventeen years old when the war broke out. Both Ian and Betty had already left the village: Ian was serving with the British Army in India and Betty joined the women's services. Dolly was still too young for military service, so she went to work in an ammunition factory in Birmingham. Dolly remembers that Auntie Jessie was "worried sick all that time" because of the bombing. In every letter to Dolly, Auntie Jessie would write, "I wish you'd come home. I wish you'd come home." So, in 1941, Dolly returned to Kiltarlity, saying she was needed on the farm.

By this time, the Canadians had arrived at Boblainy, and both the Frasers and MacKintoshes lived near enough to 15 Company's camp that they could hear the saws buzzing and the men working in the woods. The sudden arrival of the Canadian loggers was all very exciting to eleven-year-old William MacKintosh and his little sisters Peggy and Christine. William remembers that one day the soldiers just showed up and started working, building roads and a sawmill. The Canadians provided all manner of amusement to the MacKintosh children and to their parents, too. Now in their eighties, William and Peggy recall the sports day competitions, where log rolling and tree felling were huge attractions. William came to know many of the CFC men and has many fond memories, including making saws with his father out of the discarded bits from the "huge" six-foot bushman saw.

As Dolly was so close to the camp, it's not surprising that she and Charlie Gunning would meet. As Dolly recalls, they were introduced to each other at a concert in Kiltarlity by their next door neighbour, Mrs. Jeannie MacKintosh. "Auntie Jeannie," as Dolly calls her, had met Charlie when he arrived at Kiltarlity bearing a letter of introduction from Jeannie's sister, Ivey Fraser, from Hartland. On April 21, 1942, one year to the day after 15 Company's arrival at Lovat No. 2 Camp, Charlie and Dolly Gunning were married at the manse in Kiltarlity. Theirs wasn't the first marriage in the unit: Private J.L. Hayes and Miss Flora M. Anderson of Beauly earned that distinction when they were married on October 29, 1941. Others followed, including Privates K.K. Perkins, A.E. Cook, B.F. King, L.B. Kitchen, J.F. Russell, R. Henry, R.D. Green, Zoel LaViolette, and Sergeant S.R. Branch, to name a few. Even Bob Allen, Roger's friend and author of 15 Company's war diary, married overseas, prompting this little side note in the diary for April 14, 1943: "Applications for permission to marry are coming in thick and fast these days, including that of the writer, Captain R.K. Allen."

The Gunnings' marriage in April 1942 is notable because it appears to be the first in which procedure was properly followed and Permission to Marry granted by the officer in command (OC) before the couple actually married. So concerned was the OC about marriages taking place in violation of procedure that he included the following note about marriages in 15 Company Orders for June 22, 1943:

Marriages

1. The commander is concerned about the number of marriages taking place without permission or before the date on which permission becomes effective.

2. The rights to dependant's allowance is directly affected if soldiers marry without permission and that if soldier marries before the permission date is effectively, marrying without permission.

3. The earliest effective date at which an application for Dependant's allowance can be entertained is two months after the date on which permission is given.

Dolly remembers that Major Williams wanted the bride and groom to get married in the camp, there being a competition of sorts between the companies to have the actual ceremony on site. But Dolly wanted a real wedding in a church, and her wishes prevailed. Major Williams didn't get his wish for a wedding at the camp, but the birth of Charlie's and Dolly's first child on April 14, 1943 was among the first for 15 Company in Scotland, and news of baby Eva made it into the company's war diary: "A daughter was born to Pte. P.C. Gunning and his wife. The child was born at Rosedene, Inverness and was christened Eva. They live just across the way from the camp and mother and daughter have since returned home, both doing well."

As the dependents of a Canadian serviceman, Dolly and the children were entitled to one-way passage to Canada, but Dolly wasn't interested in leaving Kiltarlity. That didn't stop Mr. and Mrs. Jackson, the caretakers of the Cossar farm back in Gagetown, from trying to convince the young couple to move to New Brunswick. The Jacksons had taken over the farm after Dr. Cossar died in 1942: the ship he was on was torpedoed and sunk; Cossar was rescued but never recovered, and the land in Gagetown went up for sale. The Jacksons purchased the entire estate, intending to re-establish assisted immigration from Scotland, and they desperately wanted Charlie and his family to come to Canada, even offering them a place to stay. In letter after letter to Dolly, they extolled the virtues of Canada and pleaded with her to emigrate. Charlie left the decision in Dolly's hands: "It's up to you," he said.

Eileen Henry, born July 3, 1943. Her mother Mary, from the Beauly area, married 15 Company's Bob Henry, from Plaster Rock, NB. War bride Mary and baby Eileen joined Bob in New Brunswick after the war.

By 1944, Dolly and Charlie had two girls born in Scotland. Meanwhile, the Jacksons continued their letter campaign, and Dolly finally relented. In March 1945, while Charlie was serving with 15 Company in Germany, she and the children made the transatlantic crossing on the *Rangitata*, a New Zealand passenger ship converted into a troopship for the war years. Dolly and the girls went to Lower Gagetown, where they lived with the Jacksons until Charlie was demobilized in fall 1945. The Gunnings had another child, a boy, and over the years they tried their hand at farming, even buying a farm with Charlie's veterans' benefits in Gordonsville, near Bristol, New Brunswick. But after a devastating house fire, they moved to St. Andrews, where Charlie worked at Bartlett's Mill. They finally settled in Woodstock, where the Jacksons had moved after selling the Cossar farm. In Woodstock, Charlie found permanent employment at the hospital, where he worked until he retired.

Dolly's sister Betty also married a 15 Company man, Private Kempton Perkins, and they, too, lived near Bristol. The sisters were two of nearly eighteen hundred war brides who came to New Brunswick after the Second World War. Dolly didn't know many of the other wives from the Beauly area, but she kept in touch with Mairi King, a friend from Kiltarlity who married a 15 Company man from the Miramichi. Mary Henry, the wife of Bob Henry of Plaster Rock, also came to New Brunswick from Beauly. The Henrys were good friends with Pat in Beauly, and he often spoke of them during the war, enclosing photographs of their first born, Eileen, in letters back home. The baby reminded him of his own granddaughter Patsy, who was born five days after he arrived in Scotland: "Lucy here is the sweet little girl you are knitting the things for. She is really bigger in the picture than she is. She is a wee little creature, but she is lovely. I can just hold her all day. I look at her and think of Paddy Ann. She has a lovely mother and Dad. Bless her little heart."

Pat's friend from down shore, Bedford Whelton, was another 15 Company man who married in Scotland. Bedford was the second-eldest of seventeen children of Edward and Louisa Whelton, third-generation Irish-Canadians whose ancestors had come to New Brunswick from County Cork and settled in Black Rock, a small Irish farming community on the northeast coast of New Brunswick between Bathurst and Grande-Anse. Bedford had just turned thirty when he joined the CFC in August 1940. When Pat arrived in Valcartier that December, he was glad to see Bedford, who had spent the fall there and knew his way around Quebec City. Bedford was with Pat on board the MS *Batory* during their trip overseas in April 1941, and he remained with 15 Company for the next four years, serving with No. 1 Canadian Forestry Group cutting logs in France, Belgium, Holland, and Germany. Bedford was nearly killed in a fire that began when he used gasoline to clean an engine at the sawmill at Kiltarlity. His friend from Bathurst, Duncan Campbell, saved his life by rolling him on the ground and putting out the flames. In May 1945, Bedford married Josephine "Joey" Keaveny in Edinburgh. Joey was from Cornagee, County Roscommon, Ireland, and, like many young Irishwomen she had left in search of better opportunities in Britain. Joey took nursing training in Edinburgh, and one day, during time off from her job as a nursing sister, she met Bedford at the Palais de Danse in Edinburgh. It was "love at first sight," said Joey in later years. When she died in 2012, the story of their first meeting in Edinburgh was told in her obituary: "He took her hand in both of his and said 'I am going to take you back to Canada'." In May 1946 Joey was on the war bride ship *Aquitania*, en route to Pier 21 in Halifax. Bedford met her at the train station in Bathurst, and they settled in Black Rock, where they established a successful dairy farm and raised seven children. The grocery store they operated doubled as the post office, and Joey became the postmistress, a prominent role for an immigrant woman in a small, rural community. Pat kept in touch with Bedford and Joey Whelton for years after the war: whenever Bedford came into Bathurst, as he often did for farm supplies or to do some shopping with Joey and the children, they stopped in to see Pat and talk about old times in Scotland.

Another 15 Company man who married a Scottish woman was Pat's good friend Zoel LaViolette. Zoel came from a large Catholic family in Nash Creek, a small village along the Bay of Chaleur between Bathurst and Dalhousie. His parents ran a mixed farm and his father was a blacksmith, an important job in a small community in the 1930s where farm implements were made by hand and horses were still the main mode of transportation. Zoel was twenty-eight years old in 1940 when both his parents died; he joined the army around the same time as Pat, and arrived in Scotland on the *Batory* along with the rest of the company in April 1941.

In Beauly, Zoel met Mairi Rattray, a much-loved teacher at the Catholic school in Eskadale. Mairi was also the church organist at St. Mary's, Eskadale, where the Lovats attended Mass. On June 12, 1944, Mairi and Zoel were married at St. Mary's, and by the end of July he was on his way to the continent with 15 Company, where he served in France, Belgium, Holland, and Germany until the company ceased operations in July 1945. Zoel returned to Canada and waited, like so many other Canadian servicemen, for his bride to follow. In Scotland, however, his friends were betting on his returning. Mary Chisholm, one of the "Femnock" Chisholms, was a nurse who worked at the Dumfries and Galloway Royal Infirmary and was a good friend of both Zoel's and Mairi's. In a letter to Pat dated December 6, 1945, Mary asks: "I wonder if Zoel will come back to this country? What about a bet?" As the eldest of nine children, Zoel would

In 1959, Zoel and Mairi LaViolette visited Pat and Bea in Bathurst, the first time they had seen each other since 1945. Here, Zoel and Mairi get ready to leave for the trip back to Nash Creek en route to Ontario: (left to right) Pat, Beatrice, Mairi, Zoel, and James.

have inherited the family farm in Nash Creek, but in the end the friendly bettors in Scotland won: he decided to return to the Highlands and try his luck there, and the Nash Creek farm went to a younger brother whose descendants still live there today.

Zoel was well liked in Beauly, and today is still remembered among the old-timers as the "beekeeper." After he came back to Scotland, he took a course in beekeeping, selling honey and providing pollination services to local farmers by transporting his bees around the countryside in a purple heather–coloured Javelin car with an attached trailer that had slots to accommodate up to twelve hives. Zoel and Mairi stayed in Eskadale until July 1954. In a Christmas letter to Pat dated December 20, 1953, Mary Chisholm says there are rumours Zoel and Mairi are planning to leave for Canada: "There is a constant rumour at present, that Zoel and his wife are leaving for Canada in the summer, whether it will materialize or not remains to be seen. Unfortunately the numbers in Eskadale school have diminished greatly and lately stood at only six. However, there is a prospect of the stray Catholics being transported to Eskadale. This may determine whether Mr. and Mrs. LaViolette remain in Scotland or not."

Unfortunately, the numbers of Catholic children at the Eskadale school did not improve, and the couple decided to seek better opportunities in Canada. Zoel and Mairi sold all their belongings at auction and left for Saskatchewan, where Mairi found a teaching position and Zoel worked as a beekeeper. Eventually, Zoel and Mairi settled in Hamilton, Ontario, where they lived the rest of their lives, Mairi working as a teacher and Zoel finding employment in the steel manufacturing industry. They bought a little cottage in Orillia, where they spent many happy times. Mairi went back to visit at least once, but Zoel never returned to Scotland. In the summer, the couple sometimes travelled to New Brunswick to visit Zoel's family in Nash Creek. In 1959, they drove the nearly sixty kilometres from Nash Creek to see their old friend Pat in Bathurst. Photos of Zoel, Mairi, Pat, and Bea show them smiling and standing alongside the car with its doors wide open, one last shot before the couple headed back home to Ontario.

Not every war bride who married a 15 Company soldier was destined to spend the rest of her life in Canada. After the war, Margaret (Simpson) Cook of Beauly lived for one year with her husband Arnett and their child in an isolated log cabin on the Sand Brook Road in Wirral, in south-central New Brunswick, before deciding that the family would be better off back in Scotland. Margaret's husband, Arnett Edward Cook, was twenty-seven years old and had been working at the Atlantic Sugar Refinery in Saint John for six months when he enlisted in the army in June 1941. Arnett was the youngest of five children of James George Cook and Margaret (née Campbell) of Saint John. The Cooks were very proud of their strong Irish roots: Arnett's great-grandfather, James Cook, was born in County Tyrone, Ireland, in 1819, and emigrated to New Brunswick as a young man. When he was 101 years old in 1919, an article about his extraordinary life appeared in the local newspaper.

Arnett was just three months old when his mother died in May 1914. His father remarried, and Arnett grew up with his father and stepmother, Ada, in Saint John, attending school there until he was just twelve. Although he could read and write, he never achieved a level of literacy that would allow him to do more than unskilled labour for the rest of his life. When Arnett was a young teenager, he moved to Wirral to live with family friends, Thelma and Vernon Mailman. Wirral was an isolated logging settlement about halfway between Fredericton and Saint John, and Arnett worked in the woods cutting lumber. In his early twenties, he did a short stint as a longshoreman, and later drove truck for two years. By the time he started working at Atlantic Sugar in 1941, a steady job in the army would have looked fairly lucrative, especially with all the young men his age joining up. After basic training in Woodstock, Arnett was sent to Camp Borden, Ontario, then to Debert, Nova Scotia, and finally Sussex, New Brunswick, before shipping out to Britain, arriving the week before Christmas 1941. Given his background in trucking, he spent the first eight months with 1 Mechanical Transport Vehicle Reception Depot, Royal Canadian Army Service Corps, at Bordon, Hampshire, England. Then, in September 1942, he was sent to the Reinforcement Section, CFC, where his logging experience was deemed more useful to the army than trucking. There, he was taken on strength with 15 Company at Boblainy, a move that had a major impact on his future, because it was while stationed near Beauly that he met his future wife, a young woman named Margaret Ann Simpson.

Margaret was one of two daughters of James and Clementina (Kinnear) Simpson, farm labourers who lived and worked on the Erchless Estate near River Beauly. Margaret was sixteen years old when she met Arnett at a New Year's Eve dance at Struy Hall in Struy, near Cannich, a small village about 32 kilometres southwest of Beauly. They fell in love, and were married, with permission, on June 8, 1943. A large wedding and reception were held at the Caledonian Hotel in Inverness: the formal portrait shows Margaret in a pretty blue dress with Arnett and his best man, Private Garnett E. Gibbons—another 15 Company man from Cross Creek, New Brunswick—both in their Canadian Army uniforms, along

Margaret Cook, in Arnett's army jacket, with rifle, daughter Pearl, and deer carcass, in front of their tarpaper shack near Wirral, NB. By Christmas 1947, the Cooks were back in Scotland. (Photo courtesy of David and Penny Cook)

with a cute little flower girl and the Rev. Alexander Boyd completing the wedding party.

Arnett crossed the Channel with 15 Company as part of No. 1 Canadian Forestry Group in July 1944, and served in France, Belgium, Holland, and Germany cutting logs for the war effort. He was granted nine days' Privileged Leave to Britain in April 1945, the first time he saw his baby daughter Pearl, who had been born in January. After 15 Company concluded operations on the continent that summer, he stayed with Margaret and Pearl at the Erchless Estate before being repatriated to Canada in August 1945. In an exit interview conducted on August 31, Arnett told the Department of Veterans Affairs that he planned to return to the Atlantic Sugar Refinery upon discharge and perhaps start up his own trucking business. But the counsellor he spoke to had doubts about the success of his plans: "Willing and eager worker, but no business man. The more logical thing for him to do is to return to his former employment and if conditions satisfactory remain there until wife arrives in Canada; then he could decide on trucking business." More than sixteen months passed before Margaret and their daughter Pearl secured passage on the war bride ship *Queen Mary* on July 26, 1946. Arnett's father had died in July 1944, so on the passenger list organized by the Canadian Wives Bureau Margaret and Pearl were officially destined for Arnett's stepmother, Ada Cook, in Saint John, but they didn't stay with Ada for long; instead, they went to Wirral, where Arnett had built a log cabin in the woods.

Coming from a small village in the Scottish Highlands, Margaret was no stranger to rural living, but she probably didn't expect to end up in a half-finished log cabin with black tarpaper on the walls and an outdoor toilet. That winter was a struggle: in photos Margaret puts on a brave face, holding a rifle with a dead deer splayed across a woodpile. But it was all too much for this young Scottish war bride. By the next Christmas, their little family was back in Scotland, where they spent the rest of their lives. With the help of his father-in-law, Arnett secured a position as a farm labourer on the Erchless Estate, where he worked for many years. He and Margaret and their growing family lived in a tithed croft, meaning they paid part of their wages back to the estate owner. When the work ended, they moved to Kilmarnock, then Struy and Lentran, and finally settled down in Culloden. Arnett never came back to Canada. In Scotland, he and Margaret raised seven children and found a permanence that evaded them in Canada. After Arnett passed away in 1976, his son David made the journey back to New Brunswick with his mother Margaret and fiancée Penny to reconnect with their Canadian relatives. In Hoyt, they visited the tiny log cabin where Arnett, Margaret, and Pearl had spent that cold winter so many years before.

Peter "Pete" and Barbara (Morrison) Pearce were another young couple whom Pat got to know very well during his time in Beauly. They lived at Glencoe House, Barbara's family home at the corner of the cobblestoned Beauly Square. Pete Pearce was a member of the Black Watch (Royal Highland Regiment) of Canada and Normandy veteran who was wounded in action in Europe. He was from Victoria, British Columbia, where his English parents had emigrated in the early part of the twentieth century. Pete was among those who went through the concentration camps at war's end, and the terrible sights he saw there gave him nightmares for years after. Peter and Pat met in Beauly through Pete's in-laws, Allan and Alexsandrina Morrison, whom Pat knew through St. Mary's Catholic Church in Beauly. In 1942, their daughter Barbara was introduced to Pete when he was in the area doing combat training.

Despite the difference in their ages, Pat became good friends with the Pearces and their names come up frequently in his letters. But Barbara's parents, Allan and Alexsandrina, were closer in age to Pat, and Pat spent time with them when he came into Beauly from Lovat No. 2 Camp at Boblainy, and later Balblair House, to attend Mass on Sundays. Both Barbara's parents were Highland Scots: her mother, Alexsandrina (MacPherson) was originally from Edderton, near Bonar Bridge, north of Inverness, while Barbara's father, Allan, was from Beauly and had been the postman, so he knew everyone in the small village. He also ran a grocer's shop where Barbara worked. After Allan became wheelchair bound, Pete was a great help, strong enough to lift Allan out of the chair and help with heavy work around the house. As lodgings were difficult to come by, Barbara and Pete lived with her parents after the young couple married in 1942. A daughter, Sandra, was born in 1943, and in 1945, Betty. Three more daughters, Christine, Evelyn, and Dorothy, followed after the war. Pat was a frequent visitor to Glencoe House, and the sudden death of Allan in late January 1945 came as a shock to his family and friends, who included Canadians from 15 Company and No. 5 District Headquarters. A small black-framed envelope and card, dated February 7, 1945, and addressed to Cpl. "Hennacy" at Balblair House, says: "Mrs. A. Morrison and family wish to return sincere thanks for the kind expressions of sympathy shown to them in their recent bereavement. Glencoe House, Beauly."

Within four months of Allan Morrison's death, the war ended, and the Pearces had to decide whether to accept or refuse the Canadian government's offer to Barbara and the girls of free transportation to Canada on a war bride ship. But Barbara didn't want to leave her widowed mother and her large extended family. In the end, the Pearces decided to raise their family in Scotland. Peter stayed on in Germany after the war, and spent two years in Berlin with the Allied Control Commission. Later, he took an accountancy course in Inverness, and formed a partnership with two other men in a transport company, Johnstone and MacKenzie, which was bought out by Charles Alexander of Aberdeen. Pete ended up working for Alexander in Peterhead, and when he retired he and Barbara moved to Kiltarlity. Pete died in 2004 and Barbara in 2009, having spent the last twenty-five years of their lives a stone's throw away from Beauly, where they met during the war.

As the marriages between 15 Company men and local women began to add up, even Pat was compelled to notice. By war's end, Pat and Bea had been married nearly thirty-five years. Privately, he admitted not all of it had been happy. In letters to Bea, he was polite and friendly, even concerned. But beneath the surface, their relationship was strained and had been for years. They had lived apart more than together, and the long separation from family during the war years didn't make it any better. Pat wrote often to his daughters Lucy and Anna. He was especially close to Lucy, his eldest daughter, with whom he shared a special bond. Recently married, Lucy was pregnant with her first child, a boy named Billy, born in August 1944, and Pat knew she would understand how he felt. In this letter, an offhand comment about 15 Company marriages and babies leads to thoughts of his own marriage and how much he misses his children now that he is getting older: "So Lucy we have a lot of babies in 15 COY now and the boys are still getting married. Some doing all right. Some not. It is a gamble any how. I hope you will be happy. For myself, home life hasn't been very happy. But we will not speak of that now. I am happy here. Only I miss you all, knowing I am getting older."

Chapter Nine

The Children Left Behind

Pat Hennessy wasn't the only man in 15 Company with a wife and family in Canada, but he was one of the oldest—and likely one of a very few with children of his own in the military, not to mention two grandchildren born in Canada during his time overseas. In 15 Company's war diary, the marital status of every recruit is duly noted, and it seems that for every single man who was taken on strength, a married one joined as well. How relations between husbands and wives fared during the long wartime absence had as much to do with one's attitudes toward the institution of marriage as it did the circumstances in which men and women found themselves after four years of separation. Most married couples were faithful to each other, but, given social attitudes toward sex education and lack of access to birth control, it's not surprising that an estimated twenty-three thousand children were born out of wedlock to Canadian servicemen, including men from 15 Company, and British women during the war.

Alfred Blizzard was married with four children when he joined the Canadian Forestry Corps in late December 1940. Alfred was from Tracy, a small community about thirty kilometres from Fredericton, along the North Oromocto River. He worked at the Fraser Mill on the Lincoln Road in Fredericton, where he was the "saw doctor." The saw doctor performs a critically important role in a sawmill, repairing, sharpening, and fit-

Fredericton Junction's Alfred Blizzard Sr., saw doctor of 15 Company, met Chrissie Fraser at a dance in Beauly; their daughter Rosie was born in August 1945.

(Photo courtesy of Rosie (Fraser) Nixon)

ting the huge blades, fixing broken teeth, maintaining saws, and helping operators troubleshoot faults. A good saw doctor was worth his weight in gold, and Alfred had a reputation as one of the best in the Saint John River valley. His eldest son, Alfred Jr., who was just twelve years old when his father went off to war, remembers that his dad was in big demand in New Brunswick: once, a sawmill in Woodstock had to shut down when his father couldn't get there on time to fix the blades. Major Williams needed a reliable man he could count on in Scotland, but Alfred wasn't going to drop everything to join the CFC without some guarantees.

Alfred had no military experience, yet he wanted assurance that he would get a sergeant's rank and pay before committing to the CFC. Major Williams agreed, and on December 29, 1940, Alfred enlisted in Fredericton. He went to Valcartier for training, and in April 1941 was onboard the MS *Batory* en route to Scotland with the rest of 15 Company. One month later, he was promoted to lance corporal, and by August he was a corporal making Trades Pay B at $2.20 a day. Within eight months, he finally got his promotion when he became a sergeant at a rate of $2.95 per day. Alfred's work as saw doctor saw him moved around between companies: his pay-book reflects his work assignments with 15 Company, then 21 Company, back to 15 Company, and then to 18 Company. Alfred Jr. recalls his father's saying that the distances between mills in Scotland were so great that he had a driver to take him around to No. 5 District different camps.

Like many other Forestry Corps men stationed near Beauly, Alfred came in contact with the staff at the Lovat Estate, including Christina "Chrissie" Fraser, the daughter of "Willie the Moon," the much-loved lightkeeper at Beaufort Castle. So highly thought of was Willie the Moon by the Lovat family that when Willie, his wife, and children, including Chrissie, emigrated to Canada in the 1920s, the 16th Lord Lovat, or "MacShimidh," as he was called, coaxed Willie back to Beauly by offering to pay their return fare, which would have been a large sum in those days. Estate workers at Beaufort Castle were normally offered tenancy of houses as part of their employment contract: the majority stayed at Old Downie, but, as a sign of his importance, Willie the Moon was given the prized Brae Cottage, a magical little croft just below Beaufort Castle, where Chrissie grew up and where young Shimi, the future 17th Lord Lovat, was a frequent visitor.

Willie the Moon had a major influence on Shimi's life, shaping his outlook on nature and his relationship with the land and his Scottish ancestry—so much so that Shimi dedicated the first chapter of his 1978 memoir, *March Past*, to "Willie the Moon—Tribute to a Clansman." When Willie died in 1940, the famous Catholic poet Maurice Baring, who spent his summers at Beaufort during the 1920s and '30s as the guest of Shimi's mother, Lady Laura Lovat, wrote a poem in Willie's honour:

If you're wanting a job to be done well and soon,
The man who can do it is Willie the Moon.
He works all day and he gives of his best,
But now he is surely in need of a rest.

It's no use a calling; he's far, far away,
He's trimming the lamps on the wide Milky Way.
All the pipers in Heaven will strike up a tune
Of welcome to Willie—dear Willie the Moon.

Chrissie Fraser and baby
daughter Rosie
(Courtesy of Rosie (Fraser) Nixon)

That same year, Willie's daughter Chrissie was hired as a companion to Lord Lovat's sister Veronica in London. Veronica had fallen in love and married naval officer Alan Phipps, the son of the former British ambassador to Paris and Berlin, and they had two children. When Phipps was killed defending the Mediterranean island of Leros in 1943, Veronica and the two children, their nanny, and Chrissie returned to Beauly. (After the war, Veronica married Sir Fitzroy Maclean, who has been called the inspiration for Ian Fleming's James Bond character.) During the war, Beaufort Castle was not as Veronica would have remembered it before her marriage to Captain Phipps. The castle had been taken over by the military, and her brother Shimi, his wife Rosamund, and family lived in private quarters in the back section. There was also a hospital on site, and security was strictly enforced. Even Willie the Moon had to show his identification while going about his lightkeeping duties. Veronica and her two children rented accommodations near Beauly and Chrissie stayed with them until her own mother took ill. Later, Chrissie found work as a nanny for a doctor's family in Beauly. At Christmas 1944, Chrissie and her sister went to a dance at Kiltarlity Hall, where, despite the movement of 15 Company to France that July, there were still many Canadians from No. 5 District working on the Lovat Estate. There, Chrissie was introduced to Sergeant Alfred Blizzard, who was then saw doctor for 18 Company at Lovat No. 1, Teanacoil.

For the next six months, Alfred and Chrissie were together. Alfred even met Chrissie's mother. But just as 18 Company shut down operations and Alfred was repatriated to Canada in May, Chrissie had to face the fact that she was pregnant. The only people she could tell were the doctor, her brother, and best friend. Together, they came up with a cover story that Chrissie was moving to Norfolk, England, to work as a nanny for the doctor, who had been transferred there with his wife and family. That August 1945, Chrissie gave birth in a private hospital to a sweet little girl named Rosie. It was common practice at that time to allow unwed mothers to nurse an infant for the first few months and then give the baby up for adoption. But after six weeks, Chrissie changed her mind about Rosie. She came back to Brae Cottage with her newborn child—no doubt surprising everyone in the village, including her own mother and the Lovats—and went right back to work at Beaufort Castle.

A single mother with a Canadian soldier's child would have raised a few eyebrows in the small Highland village, but Chrissie wasn't the only one: many young Beauly women bore children out of wedlock during the war years—"little packages left behind by the Canadians," as they were called by the locals. "In those days, they just didn't talk about it," says Rosie. "So many women had babies by men in the Forestry Corps. The mothers went away, had the babies, and came back. People just didn't talk about it." But Chrissie was different. Rosie explains: "I always knew my father was a Canadian soldier. I knew about her going to England and about the people who were supposed to adopt me. She was very open about that aspect." Yet, there were some things Chrissie wasn't willing to share, and one was Alfred Blizzard's name.

The late Alfred Blizzard Jr., of Fredericton Junction, and his sister Rosie (Fraser) Nixon of Beauly, finally reunited in October 2012 (Photo by the author)

When Rosie was eight years old, Chrissie married a local man who raised the girl as his own. Rosie grew up at Old Downie, sharing a privileged upbringing with the children of Lord and Lady Lovat and wondering for the rest of her life who her real father was. Chrissie died suddenly in 1963, when Rosie was only seventeen. After the funeral, Rosie was sorting through her mother's belongings when she came across an address book with the details of A.P. Blizzard and his Canadian military personnel number. At the time, she didn't pursue the lead, thinking it would upset her stepfather. Ten years later, when he died, Rosie finally felt free to start looking for her biological father. For five years, Rosie tried to find A.P. Blizzard. She wrote to the Canadian High Commission, Veterans Affairs, the Military Personnel Unit of the National Archives of Canada, and the Royal Canadian Legion. Each one cited the *Privacy Act* as the reason

Rosie could not obtain information about the man. Rosie even contacted organizations that help reunite Canadian veterans with their long-lost children, but they, too, couldn't get anywhere in Ottawa. In a final act of desperation, she and her cousin Richard Fraser, who worked in London and had access to Canadian telephone books through his work, phoned all the Blizzards in the Fredericton telephone book. They got nowhere. In 1988, Rosie gave up.

Unknown to Rosie, Alfred Blizzard's family back in Fredericton knew all about the little girl in Scotland; they just didn't know her name or where she lived. It seems that Alfred's brother Lemuel, who served with him in 15 Company during the war, had a crisis of conscience one night after he returned from overseas, and told Alfred's wife Edith about the baby back in Scotland. In the late 1950s, when Alfred Jr. and his brother were in their early thirties, they visited Beauly while on a trip to Britain with their wives. In the back of their minds was the faint hope that they might find the girl. With little or no information to go on, they didn't get very far. Wishful thinking about their half-sister back in Scotland kept the story alive, even after their father passed away in the 1980s.

It took nearly sixty-five years, but in 2012 Rosie traced her father's family to Fredericton, and with the help of modern DNA techniques was able to prove without a doubt that she was the child of Alfred P. Blizzard, the saw doctor of 15 Company. Since then, Rosie has been to Fredericton twice to meet Alfred Jr. and her other half-siblings, including a sister with whom she has become very close. While in New Brunswick, she was introduced to the extended family and visited her father's grave in Tracy, putting to rest the old ghosts that had haunted her for a lifetime.

Fred Cogswell, "the poet of the unit," joined the
CFC in 1940, trained at Valcartier, and sailed to
Scotland on the MS *Batory* with Pat and the rest of
15 Company in April 1941. (Photo courtesy of Kathleen Forsythe)

Chapter Ten

Fred Cogswell, Poet of the Camp

Lucy I got a bicycle. Me and the bookkeeper of the Major's.
His name is Sergeant Cogswell. It does us fine.
   —Patrick Hennessy to Lucy Hennessy, August 20, 1941

In August 1941, Pat Hennessy and Sergeant Frederick Cogswell pooled their resources and bought a bicycle. Bicycles were a popular mode of transportation for the Forestry Corps because, other than walking, there was no way to get to the surrounding villages of Kiltarlity, Eskadale, or Beauly. A bicycle gave one independence and a means of travel around the countryside on days off. For Pat, the bike was especially important because he wanted to go to church on Sundays and St. Mary's, Beauly, was six miles away: "Thank god I get to mass every second Sunday," he wrote to Bea. "I go on my bike."

Pat and Fred Cogswell likely met in the little stone farmhouse that had been converted into the officers' mess soon after 15 Company arrived at Boblainy. Pat had been cooking for the officers since June 1941, and, as one of fourteen sergeants in the company, Fred would have had reason to go to the mess from time to time. He worked for the commanding officer, Major Williams, having moved up the ranks fairly quickly because of his education and writing ability. Although Pat probably never knew it, his CFC friend Fred Cogswell went on to become one of Canada's foremost poets. As a tribute to the important role Fred played in the development of the literary arts in Canada, his life story has been documented by Dr. Tony

A bicycle was often the only way soldiers living in remote Highland camps could get around. Pat and Fred Cogswell bought one together in 1941 to get to Beauly, Kiltarlity, and Eskadale.

Tremblay in the digital volume *Fred Cogswell: The Many-Dimensioned Self.* Described as "both a Selected Works of Cogswell and a Critical Appraisal of his creative and cultural work, ... it offers a broad entry to and assessment of the work of one of Canada's most important literary modernists." It also contains a detailed biography of Fred's early years, his ancestry, education, and military service, and was an invaluable source for this chapter.

Fred grew up near Centreville, New Brunswick, where his father ran a mixed farm in Cogswell's Settlement — so-named after his American Cogswell ancestors, who settled on lands vacated by the Acadians after 1760. Fred descended from a colourful line of Acadians and Puritans, an unusual combination by any account in rural, west-central New Brunswick. His grandmother, Marie Elizabeth Girouard of Bouctouche, came from a prominent Acadian family: her father, Gilbert Anselme Girouard, was the member of Parliament for Kent County, a strong proponent of Acadian rights, and a favourite of Sir John A. Macdonald,

Canada's first prime minister. Elizabeth was also the first Acadian woman to receive a university degree (music) in New Brunswick. But she defied her family's expectations and, on the very night of her expected marriage to another man, ran off with Fred (LeBlanc) White, a Harvard-educated veterinarian. Elizabeth and Fred escaped to Rivière-du-Loup, Quebec, across the border from New Brunswick. Later, they moved to Bath, New Brunswick, far enough from the prying eyes and admonitions of Elizabeth's Kent County relatives.

All was not well, however, in the White household. After the birth of their seventh child, Fred faked his death to start a new life with another woman in Bathurst, where he set up a successful veterinary practice. Now abandoned and with seven children to care for, in 1916 Elizabeth married off their teenaged daughter Florence to a local farmer, thirty-four-year old Walter Scott Cogswell, a Baptist who worked the land that had been in his family since 1810. He is described as a "conservative" and "argumentative" man who shunned modern farming methods and technology. He refused to buy into the rural electrification program espoused by New Brunswick premier R.B. McNair in the 1940s, and ploughed his fields with a horse long after his more successful neighbour, A.D. McCain, bought a tractor.

Fred, their first child, was born in 1917. He attended school in Centreville and loved baseball, but a speech impediment made him a target for bullies. He withdrew into a kinder world of reading and writing, encouraged by his mother, who wanted Fred to escape the farm through education. In 1935, when he was eighteen years old, he went to Normal School in Fredericton, where he obtained a first class teacher's licence. He taught high school for two years at Gordonsville and Hartley Settlement, but was ill-suited for teaching teenaged boys and lost both jobs. As Dr. Tremblay writes, when Fred "asked Mr. Waugh, his old principal at Centreville Superior School, for advice, he was told to hit the larger boys over the head with the book while saying 'let that sink in.'" Instead, Fred left teaching and set his sights on a career in the diplomatic service, enrolling in Carleton County Vocational School, where he took clerkship and accounting, and graduated with a commercial diploma in 1939. But world events—and a bureaucratic error·

Fred Cogswell, on the steps of
15 Company's orderly room,
Camp Valcartier, March 1941
(Photo courtesy of Kathleen Forsythe)

that saw his application for the diplomatic service rerouted to the wrong
government department — led him to join the army.

By December 1939, the first contingent of Canadian servicemen was
already in England, among them many local men known to Fred who
had joined the Carleton and York Regiment. Their letters back home
describing their adventures overseas appeared in the local newspaper,
the *Victoria Gazette*, and they inspired Fred to enlist. One cold February
day in 1940, Fred left Woodstock and walked the ninety kilometres to
Fredericton with the intention of joining the infantry. It took him two
days, with a stopover at a cousin's house along the way. When he arrived
in the capital, he discovered that a poem he had written about the German
invasion of Poland had been published in the Saint John *Telegraph Journal*.
It was his first published work.

To his good fortune, Fred was not accepted into the infantry — bad
eyesight and broken fingers from a childhood of catching baseballs bare-
handed put an end to that plan. Six months later, in August 1940, he was

medically re-examined and classified "A." On August 16, he was sent to 15 Company, where his skills could be put to good use as a clerk. Fred came into the company just as the unit was being formed. There were still a lot of details to work out and plenty of opportunity for an educated man. He was taken on strength as a private on August 19, and the next day promoted to sergeant. From 15 Company Headquarters in Chatham, the unit went to Quebec for basic training in October. Save for a two-week furlough in February 1941, Fred stayed in Quebec with the unit until its departure for Scotland in April on the MS *Batory*.

Fred's work ranged from manning the switchboards and maintaining an inventory of the lumber cut each day to typing up routine orders. In his letters back home, Pat describes Fred as a "clerk" who works for Major Williams, so it is entirely possible that Fred, with his background in writing, also wrote 15 Company's war diary. This early entry about Major Matthews, the Canadian Legion education officer, seems to be the work of someone with an admiration for literature:

> The company has recently received a library from the Canadian Legion through the efforts of Major Matthews, Educational Officer attached to the Forestry Corps. Consisting of 100 well bound volumes of good fiction, mystery, etc., all by well known and popular authors, the library is being made good use of by all ranks of the company. It is a pleasure to record in this diary a word of appreciation for the work being done by Major Matthews in his capacity as Educational Officer for the Canadian Legion War Services. His duties take him to all the 20 companies at present comprising the Canadian Forestry Corps, and widely scattered over all of Scotland. His advice and encouragement has meant much to the numerous men in uniform interested in advancement and self-improvement through studies in their spare time.

In March 1943, Fred was transferred to No. 2 District Headquarters at Struan Lodge, in Aboyne, almost 150 kilometres south of Beauly and

MS *Batory* in peacetime: this vessel took Pat and 15 Company to Scotland in April 1941. (Public Domain, image from Wikimedia Commons)

48 kilometres west of Aberdeen. As one of the original 15 Company's non-commissioned officers, Fred was well liked by his peers, and his departure earned this mention in the company's war diary: "The poet of the unit, G.17024 Sgt. Cogswell, F.W., left to-day [*sic*] for fields of greater inspiration around the Deeside. He is to be Superintending Clerk at No. 2 District between poems." As Dr. Tony Tremblay notes in *The Many-Dimensioned Self*, the tasks Fred was given as "superintending clerk" were monotonous and not very inspiring. In one of his poems, "Three Legs," he writes: "Instead of poems I wrote / Part II Orders, skeleton's [*sic*] of War's truth.... Inside myself the world I made was dead." Nevertheless, Fred's military service in Scotland has also been described as the best time of his life. In Scotland and England, he could attend lectures organized by Major Matthews through the Canadian Army Educational Services. He even had a poem published in *Chambers's Journal* from Edinburgh.

It was during one of Fred's furloughs down south to Exeter that he met his future wife, Margaret "Pat" Hynes. Margaret was originally from Ireland,

and was a trained nurse who had been working in England for four years. In July 1944, they were married and in August 1945 Fred was repatriated back to Canada. Their first child, a daughter Carmen, was born that September, and a full year passed before Pat and Carmen joined him in Centreville, arriving in Halifax in August 1946 on the *Queen Mary* with thousands of other Canadian war brides. Meantime, Fred took full advantage of the veterans' rehabilitation grants that included one month tuition for every month's service, enrolling at the University of New Brunswick in September 1945. The generous veterans' program enabled him to obtain a bachelor of arts (1949) followed by a master of arts (1950) at UNB and then a PhD at the University of Edinburgh (1952). It was during this time that Fred also became involved in politics, first with the Co-operative Commonwealth Federation and later the New Democratic Party. Fred had wanted to do his PhD at Oxford and had applied for a Rhodes Scholarship, but his left-leaning politics put an end to that dream when, during the interview, he said he would never change his political views.

In 1952, Fred joined the English Department at UNB, becoming professor emeritus in 1983. He was a prolific writer, editor, translator, and scholar, publishing over forty titles of his own work. In 1981, he was awarded the Order of Canada for his contribution to Canadian literature and his work as a translator of French-Canadian poetry. Fred was credited with influencing thousands of students during his thirty years at UNB as the editor of *The Fiddlehead* magazine and publisher of Fiddlehead Poetry Books. When he died, obituaries appeared across Canada calling him a mentor and friend to hundreds of poets and writers.

Although his Scottish experience did not define Fred's writing career, it was woven into several poems in his vast collection, with more than a dozen referring to Scotland during the war, including "Circular Saws," a commentary on the physical and emotional scars that a circular saw can leave behind, and "The Fifth Christmas," about attending midnight Mass at a Polish camp in Scotland. Included in the Scottish poems is "G17024," a play on Fred's service number, which, in a roundabout way, gives credit to the Forestry Corps for his later success as one of Canada's most influential poets:

In 1940 the lottery was war,
My ticket number G17024,
And then it was I staked my puny claim
With a cipher more meaningful than name.
The prize was peace and freedom for us all,
The odds that favoured victory were small,
But yet when 1945 came around
The unexpected happened and I found
Myself secure in new civilian dress
And had at last for very own, no less,
What I had lacked for many years, a will
With which to steer my life. I have it still.
And when that happened, G17024,
As if it had not been, was then no more.
But now, after years of being free,
In age I find that number haunting me.

Chapter Eleven

Oxford University

Lucy I am going to London the 29th on leave and I am taken a 6 day course at Oxford University. Won't that be grand. It is a tour of lectures. Some of our boys been to it. Major Mathews wants me to go so I am. I will write you all about it later.
— Patrick Hennessy to Lucy Jarratt, October 18, 1943

In early November 1943, Pat attended a week-long "course" at Balliol College, Oxford, a far cry from the one-room schoolhouse in Blackville, New Brunswick, where he had managed to scrabble together a grade three education. But with the encouragement of Major Matthews, the education officer for the CFC, Pat applied to the Canadian Legion Army Services for permission to enrol and was accepted. The cost: £1.12s.—about $3 in today's Canadian currency.

The opportunity to take courses at Balliol College was likely connected to Pat's close friendship with officers in 15 Company and No. 5 District Headquarters. Thinking Pat a likeable enough fellow, Major Matthews decided it would be good for him to get an education in British history. It helped that Pat was a good cook, and perhaps they felt he deserved special treatment for the excellent meals he was providing, not only for them, but for all the other officers from camps in the district. Certainly Pat was astute enough to warrant this observation of his own cooking skills in this letter to Lucy: "You know Lucy, here I am cook for the officers. I meet a lot of officers from other companys and one gets to know people. You bet I cook them some good old feeds. They say, 'Let's go to No 15 to get a good feed.' And it's no joke for we have plenty and Mr. Allen is so good. He is messing officer."

Formation Education Officer,

Cdn Forestry Corps

Canadian Army, England.

To: G 48191 Pte. Hennessey P.J.

No 15 Coy C.F.C.

T COURSE AT OXFORD UNIVERSITY
Commencing   1 November 43

1.   Your application for the m/n Canadian Legion Educational
Services course has been accepted and your enrolment has been
carried out.

2.   Not later than 1800 hrs. on Monday   1 Nov 43
you will report at BALLIOL COLLEGE.

3.   Leaving the G.W.R. station keep to the left past the L.M.S.
station.   Now turn sharp left (past the Railway Hotel on your
right), turn right along Hythe Bridge Street, over Hythe Bridge,
cross the intersection (traffic lights), continue up George Street,
cross the main road (traffic lights) into Broad Street.   Enter
Balliol College by the first DOUBLE DOOR on your left.

4.   At the Porter's Lodge you will find a letter directing you
to your room.

5.   The all inclusive cost is £ 1.12.0 payable on arrival.

6.   IMPORTANT NOTICES:-
        (i) Attach your pass to these joining instructions.
        (ii) Please bring your RATION CARD, towel and soap.
        (iii) Kindly acknowledge receipt of these joining
        instructions to Formation Education Officer,
by letter or by telephone   AND IF YOU FIND
THAT YOUR ATTENDING THIS COURSE IS LIKELY TO BE PREVENTED LET HIM
KNOW AT ONCE.
        (iv) If within 48 hrs before the opening of the course,
you find that you cannot attend, please notify the u/m by telegraph
Alington, Balliol College, Oxford.

7.   Although enrolment in leave courses is voluntary the
University Authorities assume that you will take part in all
activities arranged for the week, and that you will co-operate
with them in every way.

8.   TO WHOM IT MAY CONCERN:- The bearer has permission to
proceed to the m/n course. It may be necessary for him to travel
during the week-end.

(Formation Education Officer)

20 Oct 43

Major Matthews, Formation Education Officer, CFC, approves Pat's
attending a six-day Tour of Lectures at Balliol College, Oxford, November 1943

The idea for the courses came from Dr. A.D. "Sandie" Lindsay, master of Balliol (1924-49) and former vice-chancellor of Oxford University (1935-38). Lindsay was an inspirational character who in his day was regarded as a dangerous revolutionary by some of his colleagues. An avowed socialist who came to national prominence during the 1926 General Strike, he was an educational advisor to the Labour Party, and helped set up unemployment clubs during the Depression. Lindsay is best known for his strong opposition to appeasement and having stood in the 1938 Oxford by-election as the anti-Munich candidate. During the Second World War he was chairman of the Joint Recruiting Board, responsible for conscientious objectors. At the end of the war, on the advice of Clement Attlee, the new post-war British prime minister, he was made 1st Baron Lindsay of Birker, of Low Ground. But Lindsay is also remembered for the important role he played in adult education at Oxford, particularly education for the armed forces.

Pat had a chance to meet Lindsay when the latter made the opening remarks and gave a lecture on "Education" at the Tour of Lectures that November. If the following description of Lindsay by one of his contemporaries is any indication, the master of Balliol would surely have left an impression on the lumberman from Bathurst: "[Lindsay] was a tall, shambling, bear of a man. Wisps of white hair floated round a large innocent pink head. He lectured in a light, sing-song voice, twisting the ends of his gown in front of him."

Lindsay might have inspired the educational courses for members of the armed forces, but their administration was through a university committee and the War Office. It seems very little is known about the wartime courses, as they were not actually part of the Oxford curriculum. And as much as course participants were thrilled to say they attended Oxford University, they were not bona fide members of the Oxford college system.

According to the Balliol Archives, the courses

> each ran for about a week, comprising lectures on aspects of English life and culture, discussions and social events. Some seventy or eighty servicemen [and -women], mostly

American and Canadian but with a sprinkling of British and other nationalities, attended each Course.

There were only short breaks between Courses, and several thousand people had passed through the College in this way when the programme ended in October 1945. The drive and finance came from the Westminster Fund, a private trust for the promotion of Anglo-American understanding, of which Lindsay was a trustee; local administration was in the hands of a Committee chaired by him, with Giles Alington of University College as coordinator. Two Balliol dons were regularly involved as lecturer: M.R. Ridley and J.N. Bryson. Every effort was made to make those attending feel that they were welcome, and in that they had joined the College in a small way, as indeed the certificates they were given on departure implied.

As much as the Tour of Lectures provided a welcome escape for service-men and women, the reality of war made it necessary for everyone to comply with blackout regulations and be prepared to defend the college from fire bombs. In a letter that Pat received with his welcome package when he arrived at Oxford was a note about "Firewatching":

Since so much of the College is occupied by members of the course, it is necessary to ask some of you to take part in the defence of the College in the event of an air raid. This involves getting up at the siren and reporting to the Chief Warden in the North-East corner of the garden quadrangle to the right of the Hall....I will assume that you will take part in this duty unless I hear to the contrary.

Giles Alington,
Secretary,
Oxford University Courses for American, Canadian and British Forces

Postcard from Oxford sent to Pat by his friend, George Graham,
a schoolmaster in Newcastle, NB, in peacetime

From Monday, November 1, to Saturday, November 6, Pat learned
the finer points of British history from some of the most highly respected
lecturers of the time, including Dr. Lindsay, Professor Arthur Leman
Goodhart, KC, an American-born British academic jurist and lawyer
who was professor of jurisprudence at Oxford, and Dr. H.G. Hanbury
of Lincoln College. Other lecturers included Field Marshal Lord
William Birdwood of Anzac, the former commander-in-chief of India,
as well as Dr. C.K. Allen, warden of Rhodes House, Oxford. "English
and American Character," "The Law Courts," "Local Government,"
"What Is Democracy?" as well as the histories of India and Oxford
University were some of the courses offered during that week. Evening
attractions for participants included dancing and dinner at Rhodes House
—built in 1928 and named after Cecil Rhodes, founder of the Rhodes
Scholarships—as well as musical entertainment organized by the noted
British music authority, Miss Margaret Deneke, and held next to Lady
Margaret Hall in Oxford.

Pat wasn't the only soldier from New Brunswick to attend Oxford, but he would have been an exception: a private — a cook, no less — without the benefit of an elementary school education attending the Oxford Tour of Lectures must have set him apart. Of the sixty-one men in the course that November, there were lieutenant-colonels, majors, captains, flying officers, and sergeants, most of whom would have come from different worlds in terms of education and class.

George Graham, a friend of Pat's from Newcastle, New Brunswick, who was a schoolmaster in peacetime, also attended the courses at Oxford. George sent Pat colour postcards from the college showing where he was billeted and had taken classes. The postcards were then forwarded to Bea in New Brunswick for her growing collection. Father Hickey also took part in the Tour of Lectures, and wrote glowingly about it in his book *The Scarlet Dawn*:

> You'd never think I was an Oxonian. Well, that I am, and a clever one. I went through Oxford in two weeks! See, it happened this way: That great university opened its doors to all army men who wanted to follow the short summer course. I took advantage of it and a more interesting two weeks I have yet to spend.
>
> The University of Oxford is a city in itself. It is made up of twenty-five colleges, each a thing of beauty and large enough to make a good sized university. There is no finer sight than the towers and spires of Oxford rearing themselves heavenward like sculptured sign posts along the hilly road to Parnassus. I stayed at Christ Church College in a room that would be classed as "rugged" in our modern colleges, but it had what makes Oxford, Oxford — age and tradition. The big heavy door with its hand-turned hinges, the low ceiling, the old-fashioned fireplace and the massive oak table take you back o'er the centuries, away from this tinsel present, and you seem to mingle with the great ones of the past. The guide draws your attention to a rough stone foundation that dates

back to the seventh century; we had our meals in a dining hall constructed by Henry the Eighth; we were shown the small lawn where the real Alice of "Alice in Wonderland" used to play; but I got the greatest thrill in the Church of St. Mary's; there I stepped into the pulpit used by Cardinal Newman when he preached the famous sermons as rector of that church.

Who would have thought that the logging camp cook with a grade three education would find himself in Oxford, one of the most prestigious universities in the world? Certainly not his friends and family back in Bathurst, who would have to be convinced with the actual letters from Oxford showing the course outline.

At the end of his nine days' leave, Pat visited Don and Hannah Fraser and their two sons William and Simon at their cottage in Old Downie on the Lovat Estate. He must have spoken to them about Oxford, and in his modest way downplayed what surely was an overwhelming experience for a country boy from New Brunswick. In a Christmas letter to Bea dated November 23, 1943, Hannah has this to say about Pat and his trip to Oxford: "He had a nice quiet rest down Oxford but he is always glad to get Home to Scotland. He says he wouldn't give one hour in Scotland for a week in England." The documents from Oxford were long ago pasted into a scrapbook that was found in the attic of the Hennessy family home in 2008. Listed alongside more than sixty senior officers and enlisted men from the Canadian, American, and British army, navy, and air forces appears the name "Pte. P.J. Hennessy" of New Brunswick.

Rothesay Collegiate School Graduating Class, 1933

Alleyne Hubbard (second from right, front row) graduating from
Rothesay Collegiate School, 1933; Sidney Jarratt, Pat's son-in-law,
stands behind him (far right, second row).

Chapter Twelve

Alleyne Hubbard, an Irreplaceable Loss

We have a new officer now. He is Lt. Alleyne Hubbard. He went to school at Rothesay with Sidney and says to say hello for him.
—Pat Hennessy to Anna Hennessy, September 17, 1942

In late August, 1942, a young forester from New Brunswick arrived at 15 Company. In the friendly atmosphere of the officers' mess, it didn't take Pat long to figure out a personal connection to Lieutenant Alleyne Hubbard through his son-in-law, Sidney Jarratt. Alleyne and Sidney had attended Rothesay Collegiate School in Rothesay, New Brunswick, graduating together in 1933. Pat was quick to send the news about Lieutenant Hubbard to Sidney in Bathurst.

Alleyne Hubbard was born on June 21, 1915, in Burton, New Brunswick, one of three children of Robert D. Wilmot Hubbard, a prominent farmer and lumberman in Sunbury County who owned a sawmill and a cooperage for making apple barrels. Alleyne came from a long line of influential Loyalists and politicians who had played a major role in the establishment of New Brunswick in 1784 and Canada in 1867. As the eldest son, Alleyne was expected to follow in the steps of his great-grandfather, the Hon. Robert Duncan Wilmot, one of New Brunswick's Fathers of Confederation. These were big shoes to fill. R.D. Wilmot had many accomplishments, among them speaker of the Canadian Senate and member of Sir. John A. Macdonald's cabinet. He ended a long life in politics as the sixth lieutenant-governor of New Brunswick. "Belmont House," the home he built in 1820 in Lincoln, near Fredericton, is now a National Historic Site.

Alleyne Hubbard was one of four forestry degree graduates from UNB in 1937. His classmate Bob Allen found work with Bathurst Power and Paper, then enlisted in the CFC, while Alleyne joined the Newfoundland Overseas Forestry Unit. They were reunited in Scotland in August 1942, when Alleyne enlisted in the Canadian Army and was sent to 15 Company. (Archives & Special Collections, UNB Libraries)

Rothesay Collegiate School was where the sons of well-to-do and prominent New Brunswickers were assured a solid English private school education. In 1933, Alleyne enrolled in the forestry program at the University of New Brunswick in Fredericton, and during the summer he worked in the woods on lumber operations in Quebec and New Brunswick. He was also a sergeant major in the Cadet Corps and manager of the UNB football team. In 1937, Alleyne graduated from UNB, but with the Depression still under way there were few jobs in forestry, so Alleyne went to Newfoundland, where he worked for Bowater at Corner Brook, cruising for wood in remote areas and working the spring logging drive.

In November 1939, the British government asked Newfoundland to form a labour force to cut pit props for use in coal production. During the First World War, Newfoundland had established a military unit called the Newfoundland Forestry Corps, and the British were eager to see a similar arrangement developed this time around. But given the urgency of the situation and the vital role that coal production played in the war effort, a civilian Newfoundland Overseas Forestry Unit (NFU) was established for immediate dispatch to Britain. On November 17, 1939, the Newfoundland commissioner for resources announced in a radio broadcast the decision to recruit two thousand loggers for timber operations in Britain. As a young forester with experience in Newfoundland and the military, Alleyne was one of four superintendents hired to recruit loggers for the NFU. By December, the first contingent of three hundred men was en route to Britain, and by January 1940 the request for two thousand had been exceeded by more than one hundred and fifty. Over the course of the next two months, another eighteen hundred men would follow in four separate sailings destined for Liverpool, the last group leaving on February 1 under the command of Superintendent Alleyne Hubbard.

From Liverpool, the NFU made its way to Scotland, where four logging districts were established, giving the NFU more than a year's head start on the Canadian Forestry Corps, the majority of which arrived only in spring 1941. Twenty-five-year-old Alleyne became superintendent of the NFU's No. 2 District Headquarters, which comprised the area south of Inverness to the Grampian Mountains. Based out of Carrbridge, Alleyne lived in the Carrbridge Hotel, which would have been quite a change from the remote logging camps he was used to in Newfoundland. Also new to him was the state of the Scottish forest, which, in letters to his parents back home in Burton, he describes as quite unlike anything he had ever seen before: "I am starting a new camp in a forest that has been very well looked after. I think they must have lived around each tree for years after the wood was planted. All the trees are straight long and about 15 inches on the stump. Not a bit of brush growing anywhere. The limbs all pruned off and the ground as level as the floor. A person could walk through it in sandals without scratching his ankle."

In summer 1940, with the air battle over Britain just beginning, Alleyne saw plenty of excitement in the skies near Carrbridge:

> Things are fairly lively around here now. We have had two air raids in the last two days. A bomb dropped about three miles from where I am staying and five more fell scattered over a radius of 8 miles. The night the bomb fell I was up on the hills patrolling for suspected parachute troops. A German plane came over and I could hear him dropping the bombs distinctly. I think he was trying to get an express train on her way south, because when she went by me she must have been going fully 70 miles per hour. It was rather humorous because it seemed to me like a hawk chasing a rabbit. The train was certainly travelling fast and letting out a whistle every so often like a frightened shriek. The bombs did no damage except break down one of the wells on the McIntosh estate which was built in 1300 and something.

In September, Alleyne testified at a highly publicized homicide trial in the High Court of Judiciary at Inverness. The victim was Newfoundlander Maxwell Hawkins, a clerk with the NFU who was a passenger in a car that was shot at by a sentry on the road outside a military camp between Grantown and Carrbridge in July. Charges against the accused were dropped after it was shown that he was acting under orders, but the trial gave Alleyne a front row seat to justice, Scottish style:

One of our boys was shot and killed in July and the trial of the man who did it came off last week. I happened to be called as one of the witnesses and was in the witness stand for about a half hour. The trial was held in the High Court Inverness and the judge came in with all the high pomp and grandeur that you read about with an escort of soldiers with scarlet tunic followed by lesser dignitaries bedecked in scarlet robes, ermine wraps etc. The members of the court all wore wigs and the judge sat with all his dignity on a sort of raised dais decked in scarlet robes and an ermine wrap. When the court was opened trumpets were blown by two pages and then settled down to business. One thing which struck me very forcibly was the order kept in court. Nobody, spectator or otherwise, moved a chair, whispered or showed any emotion. In fact, when the lawyer or witnesses were not speaking you could hear a pin drop. It was indeed quite a new experience for me.

Alleyne worked with the NFU for two and a half years before joining the Canadian Army. He could have stayed with the Newfoundlanders — the NFU was in Scotland until 1946 — but there were some practical issues to consider. Alleyne intended to marry an English woman, Sybil Strickland, whom he had met overseas. The plan was to return to New Brunswick after the war, buy his uncle Woodbridge Hubbard's farm in Burton, start a family, and establish a business. Meantime, as his father, Robert D. Hubbard, made clear, Canadian military experience would be necessary if Alleyne expected to follow family tradition and run for federal politics in York-Sunbury riding after the war.

Accordingly, on August 10, 1942, Alleyne enlisted in the Canadian Army. Because of his NFU experience, university education, and military training with the cadets, he was taken on strength as 2nd lieutenant in the

Reinforcement Section, CFC. Within five days, he was with 15 Company at Lovat No. 2 in Boblainy Forest, where he worked for the next sixteen months. The company war diary for August 21 notes his arrival: "Lt. A.R. Hubbard came to 15 COY from Reinforcement Section. Al has been with the Newfoundland Forestry Unit in this country for nearly two years. His experience in logging will be a valued addition to the Company." Whether Alleyne knew beforehand that his old UNB classmate Bob Allen, now Captain Allen, was also in 15 Company is unknown, but the friends made up for lost time: within the year, Alleyne was best man at Bob's wedding to Miss Jean MacAlpine Tate in Derbyshire, England.

Hubbard had a bright future with 15 Company. By all accounts he was well liked, personable, and intelligent. He was also a good writer: his summary of the company's forestry operations in Scotland has appeared in numerous publications, including *Sawdust Fusiliers* by William Wonders. His letters home to his family in New Brunswick show he was thoroughly enjoying military life and meeting New Brunswickers "in nearly every outfit from all over Canada."

> Today at dinner I was sitting at table with an officer from Edmonton. He seemed to be a very fluent talker and seemed to know all the answers. After talking with him I found out that his name was Grass and his people came from N'asis [Nashwaaksis]. His grandfather was Albert Grass. I think if I remember correctly that I have heard you speak of him. This chap I am talking about told me he is a cousin of Ewart Atkinson and I would quite believe it by his manners and way of speaking. He told me that he was raised up river at Perth, but he seemed to know all the people around the country, Upper Gagetown, Fredericton and other places in New Brunswick.

Ever practical, Alleyne wanted to be certain that his father had power of attorney, so he enclosed the details about his Newfoundland and Scottish bank accounts in three separate letters over several weeks to make sure that at least one reached Canada: "In case anything happens to me, you might as well have the benefit of it."

Under normal circumstances, Pat Hennessy and Alleyne Hubbard probably never would have met, but in the backwoods of northern Scotland during the Second World War, the usual social constraints of class and education didn't stop CFC men from talking to each other and sharing news from home. In January 1943, Pat sent a second message to his son-in-law Sidney, this time telling him to write to "Mr. Hubbard": "Tell Sidney he should write to Mr. Hubbard. He always asks for Sidney. They went to school at Rothesay together. He likes Sidney very much."

On April 1, 1944, 15 Company ended operations in Scotland and prepared to move to France. Pat was transferred to Balblair House, near Beauly, to cook for the officers of No. 5 District Headquarters and a group of handpicked younger men who were staying on for the expected move to the continent that summer. Alleyne was sent on more courses in advance handling and fieldcraft, as well as defence rescue training. In July, the men moved to Sussex in southern England in preparation for the journey to France. 15 Company's war diary records many bureaucratic foul-ups, frustrations, and confusion that were bound to occur when moving such a large group across the Channel in wartime. On July 26, the company landed at Arromanches, on the Normandy coast, and thus began a new chapter in the CFC's history on the European continent.

In France, 15 Company joined nine other units of No. 1 Canadian Forestry Group, whose job it was to find, cut, and deliver timber to the allies. In Scotland, the most dangerous encounters would have been like those described by Alleyne during the air war: almost "humorous," he said. But in Europe it was a very different story. The lumbermen found themselves in the middle of a war zone, and for the first time there were injuries caused by enemy fire. On the very first day, as though receiving a warning of things to come, one man was grazed by machine-gun bullets from attacking German planes, and that night shrapnel pierced some tents, just missing the sleeping men. Over the course of the next five months, 15 Company men had many near misses, but on Friday, November 20, their luck ran out. That day, Lieutenant Hubbard and his driver, Lance Corporal

Alleyne Hubbard, 15
Company, CFC
(Photo courtesy of Fred and Lucy Hubbard)

Grave of Lieutenant Alleyne
Hubbard, Groesbeek Canadian
War Cemetery, Netherlands
(Photo courtesy of Fred and Lucy Hubbard)

Eddie O'Toole of Bathurst, headed out early to Nijmegen, Holland, to discuss requirements for the Canadian Railroad Establishment, which was expected to take most of the timber from the area. O'Toole had been with 15 Company from the beginning, making his way through basic training at Valcartier, going overseas in April 1941 with Pat, on to Lovat No. 2 for three years, and then to France that July with the rest of the company. He had no reason to suspect that day would be any different. But what began as an otherwise ordinary assignment ended in tragedy when an enemy shell burst within metres of their jeep, sending a piece of shrapnel through the roof of the vehicle. O'Toole narrowly escaped injury, but Alleyne was mortally wounded. By the time they got to the nearest medical facility, it was too late. The war diary recorded the tragic details: "L/Cpl. O'Toole returned to camp at 17:15 hours and told us that Lieut. Hubbard had been very seriously injured by a German shell while in Nijmegen, adding that the Doctor who looked at him said there was no hope of recovery. It gave us all a tremendous jolt.... Here was the first of our unit to feel the sting of the ugly German war machine, a sting that was felt, not only through our own unit, but throughout the 10 companies that comprised No. 1 Canadian Forestry Group. Mr. Hubbard's loss was a very great one to our unit, an irreplaceable loss."

Nine days later, notice of Alleyne's death appeared in the Fredericton *Daily Gleaner*. "Lt. A.R. Hubbard Killed on Western Front," read the headline. "Word came this week to Mr. and Mrs. R.D. Wilmot Hubbard, Burton, that their eldest son Lieut. Alleyne Russel Hubbard, has been killed in action somewhere on the Western Front.... He had a great many friends in many parts of Canada who will learn with profound regret that he has made the supreme sacrifice." Alleyne Hubbard was buried at Groesbeek Canadian War Cemetery near Nijmegen. In 1948, his heartbroken parents received photographs of Alleyne's grave along with a letter from the family who were entrusted with tending the site.

Thankful for these small acts of kindness, the Hubbards reached out to the Dutch family and offered to help them come to Canada. One of the daughters took the Hubbards up on their offer, and she found work as a domestic in Toronto, becoming part of that great post-war immigration

In June 1950, Alleyne Hubbard's parents dedicated a stained glass window in his honour at Rothesay Collegiate School Chapel. It reads: "To the Glory of God and in loving memory of Lieut. Alleyne Russell Hubbard who attended this school from 1929 to 1933 and gave his life for his country near Nijmegen, Holland, November 20, 1944."

(Photo courtesy of Jennifer Roos, Rothesay Netherwood School)

from Holland. Her brother soon followed, and they both settled in Ontario. Alleyne's English fiancée, Sybil, came to Canada and stayed for some time with the Hubbards at their home in Burton. She moved to Montreal to live with Alleyne's sister, Marion Loggie, and there she met a Canadian whom she married. Sybil never forgot Alleyne or his family back in New Brunswick, remaining friends with the Hubbards for the rest of her life. After the war, the Hubbards ensured that Alleyne's name would never be forgotten when they established a scholarship in his honour at the University of New Brunswick. In the 1950s, the family also commissioned a magnificent stained glass window at his school, Rothesay Collegiate. On the window appears a delicate rendering of the CFC logo. Alleyne is also remembered on the cenotaphs in Oromocto and Fredericton, along with more than two dozen other servicemen who gave their lives in the Second World War.

Chapter Thirteen

A Longing for Home

Bonny Scotland it is a grand old place and the people have made us very happy. God bless them all. But now the war in Europe is over and we all have a longing for home.
—Patrick Hennessy to Lucy Jarratt, June 6, 1945

On Monday, May 7, 1945, the BBC announced the long-awaited unconditional surrender of Germany and a formal end to the war in Europe. After six years of endless fear and worry, spontaneous celebrations erupted across the globe. In Britain, the next two days were declared national holidays, and Tuesday, May 8, would be officially known as Victory in Europe (VE) Day. In Beauly, Pat, Don, Hannah, and ten-year-old Simon gathered around the radio at the Frasers' home in Old Downie, and listened to King George VI as he paid tribute to the men and women who had given their lives for victory on the land, in the air, and at sea.

Today we give thanks to Almighty God for a great deliverance.
Speaking from our Empire's oldest capital city, war-battered but never for one moment daunted or dismayed, speaking from London, I ask you to join with me in that act of thanksgiving.
Germany, the enemy who drove all Europe into war, has been finally overcome. In the Far East we have yet to deal with the Japanese, a determined and cruel foe. To this we shall turn with the utmost resolve and with all our resources. But at this hour when the dreadful shadow of war has passed far from our hearths and homes in these islands, we may

at last make one pause for thanksgiving and then turn our thoughts to the task all over the world which peace in Europe brings with it.

Let us remember those who will not come back: their constancy and courage in battle, their sacrifice and endurance in the face of a merciless enemy; let us remember the men in all the services, the women in all the services, who have laid down their lives.

We have come to the end of our tribulation and they are not with us at the moment of our rejoicing.

That evening after tea, Pat, Don, and Simon Fraser went into Beauly, leaving Hannah behind at Old Downie to entertain guests into the wee hours of the morning. William, age seventeen, the Frasers' eldest, was away working at Cape Wrath in the north of Scotland, and he missed the celebrations in Beauly. As they found out later, William had enough excitement of his own, for he witnessed the historic mass surrender of German U-boats at Loch Eriboll. When he returned to Beauly, William gave Pat a souvenir shell scooped off the beach; on it were the words "German U-Boats Surrender, Loch Eriboll, May 1945."

That night in Beauly, a giant bonfire in the village square drew a jubilant crowd for dancing and bagpipes, followed by a rare fireworks demonstration to celebrate VE Day. Afterwards, Pat visited with Pete and Barbara Pearce at Glencoe House to view the celebrations in the central square below. In a letter to Anna, Pat describes the joyful mood: "We had quite a celebration in Beauly. Fireworks and a bonfire in the square. My but the kids enjoyed themselves at the bonfire. They also had dancing on the street. Bagpipes furnished the music. I stayed until after 12 o'clock. I had tea at the Pearces at 11:30 — that was one of our boys' wife's home."

That same day, but thousands of miles away in Bathurst, Bea, Anna, Lucy, and Sidney also listened to the king on the radio in the parlour of the Hennessy home. Later, with one-year-old Billy in tow, they attended the VE Day parade, which ended with rousing speeches at the cenotaph on St. Patrick Street. V-shaped pennants affixed to telephone poles and light

Pete and Barbara (Morrison) Pearce and daughter Sandra, outside
their home, Glencoe House, 1997. The house is on Beauly Square,
next to the ruins of the ancient priory in the background.
(Photo courtesy of Betty Kokholm, daughter of Pete and Barbara Pearce)

posts along the parade route reminded everyone of the importance of the
occasion, but Bea didn't need to be reminded. She was happy. Where so
many other families in Bathurst had lost a husband, brother, or son, Bea's
husband, Pat, and their three sons, Roger, James, and Bruno, would return
to New Brunswick unscathed. Nephews Weaver Hennessy of Blackville
and Edison, Hubert, and Elbridge Hennessy of Atholville also made it
through without a scratch. Even Anna's beau, the Norwegian merchant
seaman Henrik Wesenberg, had beat the odds of repeated convoy duty in
the Atlantic and Scapa Flow and survived. There was much to be thankful
for. Soon the men would be home and life could return to normal.

It had been nearly five years since Pat joined the CFC, and although
he missed his family in Canada, he still wanted to stay on and serve with
the Canadian Army Occupation Force. This would be his last chance to

A crowd of five thousand listens to Mayor Connelly's speech at the
First World War cenotaph in front of the courthouse, Bathurst, VE Day 1945.
(P214/310, Provincial Archives of New Brunswick)

see France, Belgium, Holland, and Germany—places he had heard so
much about from his son James and friends in 15 Company who had
volunteered with No. 1 Canadian Forestry Group on the continent. In a
letter written in April 1945 to his daughter-in-law Eileen, Pat says he has
applied to serve in Europe but is prepared for what ever the army has in
store for him: "The CFC is just about finished in Scotland and we'll all
be in Canada by August. I will be going first to England to the RCASC
[Royal Canadian Army Service Corps]. I may go to the continent. I put
in for the draft and I hope to make it. Any how, if I do not I'll just take the
next best." Pat must have discussed the issue with James during his visit to
Beauly before Christmas 1944 and again in February 1945, when the young
man spent another ten days' leave with his father in the Highlands. But
even with seven years shaved off Pat's real age (then sixty-one), they both
knew a European posting was unlikely for a fifty-five-year-old army cook
with four-and-a-half years' service and a wife and family back home. In all
probability, Pat would be repatriated to Canada before the end of summer.

As the weeks passed, Hannah and Don Fraser at Old Downie were also concerned about Pat's future, wondering out loud in a letter to Bea what was going to happen to their friend, who had become like family to them in the four years since they had met in May 1941: "We are all just beginning to wonder when Pat will be moving. What we will do then, I don't know. Simon absolutely worships him." James had already figured out the obvious, and by mid-May was telling his mother in letters back home to expect "Papa" as early as August. And in a letter written about the same time to his daughter Anna, Pat had to accept that there was little chance he would see Europe because of his age: "We are still at Balblair House. We have no word about going home yet. The CFC is still cutting logs. From here I will be going to Aldershot camp. I may get a chance to go to the continent yet. I put in but they say I am too old now."

Until then, Pat seemed to live a charmed life in the army: other than a minor shoulder injury from a tumble during a blackout in 1941 and the odd bout of lumbago or rheumatism, he had been healthy for the past five years. While younger men were being cut from the ranks and sent home to Canada, Pat managed to hang on to his job. He was even promoted to corporal and offered a more comfortable position as cook for No. 5 District Headquarters at Balblair House when 15 Company was sent to the continent. Four trips to Ireland, travels to every corner of Britain, including a lecture tour of Oxford, and visits with Scottish and English friends were part of his wartime experience. Why shouldn't he go to Europe, too?

But there would be no European adventure for Pat. By the end of May 1945, he knew for certain that his time overseas would soon be over: "I will be leaving Scotland in 25th June for Aldershot camp. From there God only knows where I shall go. It will be different when I get to Aldershot. Just spit and polish. Anyhow, they never shall make a soldier out of me now." Resigned to the inevitable, he expected to be sent back to Canada in August.

As it turned out, Pat managed to extend his stay in Beauly for two more weeks before reporting to Aldershot on July 10. During that time, he was given a large, ornate iron key as a gift by Lady Lovat. We do not know the circumstances of the gift, but when Pat came back to Canada, the story

Balblair House, turned over by Lord Lovat to the Canadians; it became No. 5 District Headquarters. Pat cooked for the officers here until the end of the war.

(Photo from No. 5 District CFC, War Diary, May 1, 1943, RG 24 16, 418, Library and Archives Canada)

Pat's famous "key" from Scotland, given to him, according to family lore, by Lady Lovat as a parting gift in 1945; whether it unlocks a door to Balblair House or Beaufort Castle is unknown. (Collection of Peter Jarratt, photo by the author)

of the key became legend. It was given a place of honour on a shelf in the dining room, which was used only for special occasions. When the subject of Scotland came up, the key would be brought out, and Pat would speak with fondness of his time in Scotland with the Canadian Forestry Corps and how he came to know Lord and Lady Lovat. On the day he left Beauly, Barbara and Pete Pearce gave Pat a treasured, leather-bound book that had belonged to Barbara's late father, Allan. Pat collected many Scottish titles during his time overseas, but *Lord Lovat 1871-1933*, by Sir Francis Lindley, was one of his favourites, not only for the subject but also for the inscription that appeared on the inside front cover.

> Cpl. PJ Hennessy
> Beauly, Inverness Shire
> Scotland
> 1945
>
> In Memory of Dad and our very best wishes
>
> Mrs. Morrison Sandra Alice
> Peter and Barbara
>
> July 10, 1945

His time in Scotland over, Pat took the train from Beauly to Inverness, then on to Aldershot and the beginning of his long journey back to Canada. Before he boarded the train at Beauly Station, Pat made Hannah Fraser promise to write to Bea with news of his departure for England. This she faithfully did in a letter the following week:

> I promised Pat when he left here last week that I would write you so here is a line. We can hardly realise that Pat is gone. I think I should hear him at the door. Very often he came as I was washing up the dishes & always with a cheery smile for all. I do hope it won't be long now till he gets home as

I know he is getting a bit weary and all this grouping etc. takes such time. We saw a shot of Bruno with Pat. I think it made him home sick to see his wee boy in khaki. The four years make a difference in children. I hope he finds you not changed in spite of your worries while he was away. Wouldn't I love to see his meeting with Paddy Ann & Lucy's boy. Hope to hear soon. Love from us all to all.

Yours affectionately
Hannah Fraser

Six weeks before he left Beauly, Pat took part in one of the last official acts of the CFC in Scotland when he was present for the raising of a huge flagpole honouring the men of the No. 5 District who had served there during the war years. Pat was proud of the CFC's accomplishments in Scotland, and in a letter to his daughter Anna, he describes the monument: "For a monument for the H.Q. C.F.C. we have erected a flagpole in Beauly square. It is 75 feet tall with a concrete base. My but it is a beauty. The little town is proud of it." There is nothing about the event in the official war diaries — perhaps, in the weeks following VE Day, the erection of a monument to the CFC might have seemed unimportant in the larger scheme of things. Another consideration is that, when it came time to mark the presence of the Canadians in Beauly, most of the No. 5 District men whose names had become so familiar to the villagers were already gone, either repatriated back home to Canada or spread out on the continent among combat units or in No. 1 Canadian Forestry Group. How many people were present that day is unknown: the moment seems to be lost to living memory and no photographs have been found. Only a small article about the event appeared in a couple of Scottish newspapers, including the *Inverness Courier* of May 29, 1945: "Presentation of Flag to Beauly—The Canadian Forestry Corps have presented to the village of Beauly a flagpole over 60ft long. It has been erected at the north end of the Square opposite the Old Priory grounds. It will be a lasting memorial to the CFC who have been a long time in the district and have made themselves very popular."

In September 1945, Pat sailed to Canada on the *Duchess of Bedford*. In the exit interview conducted with every returning soldier, Pat was asked what he wanted to do. One can sense the uncertainty in his response, as recorded by the interviewer: "Undecided as to what he will do. Does not want to cook. Owns his own home in Bathurst, NB. Not interested in gardening. May sell his house because it is too big now." Pat's plans to sell the house would have been news to Bea, who, in his long absences over more than thirty-five years, had become—the man's traditional role in the family notwithstanding—the de facto head of the household, in control of all major decisions. And despite their sons' and daughter's obvious lack of interest in pursuing farming for a living, the children and grandchildren would still call the old house home for years to come. At any given point over the next twenty years, three or four of the Hennessy children, along with their wives, husbands, and families, all lived at the homestead while new homes were built for them nearby in the empty fields surrounding the old farm.

Pat could have been discharged from the army and gone home to Bathurst, but he had trouble adjusting and couldn't settle down. He decided to stay on in the military, preferring the guaranteed wage and benefits to the uncertainty of farming or cooking in the woods. Besides, the farm was no more, and things had changed so much in the forest industry that there was no going back to the way things were before. After the war, the boys all found work elsewhere. Roger and Eileen moved with their children to Toronto, where he worked as a commercial artist and draughtsman. They returned to Bathurst in the 1960s. James and Bruno both found full-time work at the mill, thanks to preferential hiring practices for returning veterans. Bobby went to St. Francis Xavier University and then Dalhousie University, where he completed his medical degree and became a doctor, setting up his practice first in Ontario, then in Bathurst. Lucy and Sidney moved out of the homestead for a few years, but they eventually came back, bringing their growing family with them. Anna and Henrik married and moved to Norway, where they stayed for eight years. They, too, came back to Bathurst out of fear of a growing Soviet threat in the Cold War years. Having survived one occupation, they were not

Bea, Pat, and daughter-in-law Frances "Fanny" (Garrett) Hennessy, James's wife, in a photo taken outside the Hennessy homestead after Pat's return to Canada in September, 1945.

willing to risk another. Henrik was hired at the mill, and they lived in the old homestead with their children for the rest of their lives.

For nearly two years, Pat worked as a cook at the military base in Moncton, until one day he collapsed in the kitchen and was found on the floor unconscious. Tests were inconclusive, but Pat couldn't go back to work. He spent the next few months at the veterans hospital in St-Anne-de-Bellevue, near Montreal, and then at Lancaster Hospital in Saint John. In January 1947, after seven years of honourable service, Pat was formally discharged from the Canadian Army. When he returned to Bathurst, he was given a job at the Woodlands Division of the Company as night watchman, a position he held until finally retiring for good in November 1955 at age seventy-one.

For more than twenty years after the war ended, letters continued to arrive from Pat's many friends in Scotland. Don and Hannah Fraser of Old Downie faithfully sent Pat Scottish newsmagazines for years. Favourite articles were cut out and ended up in the familiar wartime scrapbooks that Bea had started in 1940. John Lee and Alice wrote from Bonnyview, as did their daughter Nan from Ayr. Letters from Father Geddes in Eskadale and the Chisholms at Femnock contained news from Beauly and Kiltarlity and described the fate of the Canadian camps after the CFC left. 15 and 19 Companies' camps housed German prisoners of war and 18 Company's was turned into a displaced persons camp. For years, it was known as the "Poles Camp," for the Polish refugees who lived there following the war. Still other news spoke of the Lovats at Beaufort Castle, war brides leaving for Canada, and the inevitable changes to the small Highland villages that were part of the ebb and flow of rural life. Planting and sowing, work, weather, marriages, births, and deaths filled the pages for years. The Pallots from Montreal, the Henrys from Plaster Rock, and even Father McGuire wrote to Pat, but as the old friends started to pass away, the letters became fewer. After Pat died in 1968, the correspondence ended.

The hundreds of letters that Bea kept from Pat's service overseas — as well as those from James, Bruno, Lucy, Anna, and the myriad relatives, neighbours, and friends, both in Canada and Scotland, who wrote to the Hennessys during the war — were stored away in the attic of the family homestead in Bathurst. Carefully stuffed in boxes and hidden in the corner under a tarp, they were forgotten for nearly seventy years until 2008, when a chance search led to their rediscovery. Collectively, these letters give us unique insight into how the Second World War changed the lives of New Brunswickers, transporting some across the Atlantic to the Highlands of Scotland, where they made new friendships that lasted for the rest of their lives, and that continue today into the second and third generations. The experience for those who remained at home was no less dramatic: years of uncertainty and struggle to keep home and family together that gave way to adaptation and change as the family farm drifted into memory and sons and daughters settled into life in postwar Canada. For others, it marked a new beginning in a new place, lives forever impacted by the winds of war that blew through small towns and big cities around the world, their history not lost, as so many wartime stories have been, but found and remembered in the Second World War letters of Pat Hennessy, a logging camp cook from Bathurst, New Brunswick.

Acknowledgements

Many people and organizations helped make this book become a reality, and I would like to take this opportunity to thank them all for their assistance. Thank you to Dr. Marc Milner, director of the Gregg Centre for the Study of War and Society at the University of New Brunswick, for his support in documenting this otherwise untold part of New Brunswick's military heritage. With Marc's blessing, Matt Douglass, a summer student at the Gregg Centre, spent the better part of a week during the summer of 2012 at Library and Archives Canada in Ottawa photographing the war diaries of 15 Company and No. 5 District Headquarters, without which so many delicious nuggets of information about the CFC would never have been known. Thanks to Brent Wilson, my editor, whose encouragement and sunny optimism every time I spoke to him about my struggles finishing this book gave me the incentive I needed to keep on task at times when I felt there was no end in sight.

Thanks also to my copy editor, Barry Norris, whose fine hand smoothed out the wrinkles in this story, and to Goose Lane Editions for its continued partnership with the Gregg Centre and the New Brunswick Military Heritage series. And thanks to Bob Dallison, historian and fellow author in the series, who saw a story in my grandfather's letters.

Thanks to the New Brunswick Arts Board for financial support in the form of a Creation Category B grant, which enabled me to travel to Scotland and interview the descendants of the many Scots who had befriended my grandfather. Being on the ground in Beauly and meeting the people whose ancestors he came to know gave me a very different perspective on the Canadians in Scotland during the Second World War.

To my friend Alasdair Cameron of Muir of Ord, Scotland, thank you for your patience and gracious assistance in unravelling the many threads of the CFC story in the Highlands, and for your frequent editorial input and personal commitment to making sure the CFC's contribution to the Second World War is never forgotten. Through Alasdair's personal network of contacts, I received permission from Anne Gloag, present-day owner of Beaufort Castle, for a personal guided tour of the castle and grounds, bringing me back to the wartime Christmas Eves when the CFC men were invited to midnight Mass. Through Alasdair, I was introduced to Ron McLean, Tommy MacKenzie, and David McLean, who brought me on a tour of what remains of the former Lovat No. 2 Camp at Boblainy. Alasdair also introduced me to the wonderful people at Archaeology for Communities in the Highlands (ARCH), Scotland, who shared their groundbreaking research into the military history of the Highlands and the archaeological footprint left behind by the Canadians, including Novar House, where the Canadians would travel by lorry to transport Wrens to CFC dance halls during the war.

Thank you to my cousins Patsy Hennessy and Sharon Olscamp, who spent the winter of 2009 scanning every single letter and archival document related to our grandfather's experiences in Scotland. To Patsy, a huge thank you for your help over the years answering the endless questions, doing research, and going above and beyond to tell our grandfather's story. Thank you, too, to my brother Peter for finding the archival documents in boxes and chests and garbage bags that were stashed away in the attic of the Hennessy Estate in Bathurst and for having the foresight to save the documents when it would have been so much easier to throw them away.

Special thanks to the late Fred and Lucy Hubbard, who so graciously opened their hearts and home to me on the many occasions when I visited them to learn more about Fred's late brother, Lieutenant Alleyne Hubbard of 15 Company. Also to their daughter Liz (Hubbard) Cantlie and her husband Colin for their generous financial support of the work that went into transcribing the hundreds of pages of archival letters and nearly three thousand pages of war diaries that form the backbone of this book. Without their financial assistance, I could not have untangled the archival record of 15 Company in Beauly. Thanks also to Fred and Lucy's son Allan and Rothesay Netherwood School.

In Scotland and Canada, much thanks to the children, grandchildren, great-nieces and nephews, cousins, and in-laws who were eager to share the stories of their Scottish relatives, neighbours, and friends during the war years. These include Alice MacDonald and Duncan (and his wife Irene) Fraser of Beauly (children of John Lee and Alice Fraser); Diane MacGillivary of Inverness (granddaughter of Don and Hannah Fraser); Rosie (Fraser) Nixon of Inverness (daughter of Alfred Blizzard, Sr.); Richard Fraser, Rosie's cousin, formerly of Beauly; David and Penny Cook of Inverness and David's brothers and sisters Pearl, Jim, Roderick, Arnett, Angela, and Charles (children of Arnett and Margaret Cook); Allan Sellar of Inverness (cousin of Barbara (Morrison) Pearce; the Pearce sisters, Sandra, Betty, Christine, Evelyn, and Dorothy, (daughters of Barbara and Peter Pearce of Beauly); Jack Johnstone of Beauly (son of Lily Johnstone); Emelie Gillies of Beauly (sister of Lily Johnstone); Jessie Poleworth of Inverness (daughter of Charles Humphries); and Alma Fraser of Beauly, who lives in the croft where Hannah Fraser grew up. Thank you to Denise and Patricia LaViolette (nieces of Zoel and Mairi LaViolette) for helping to piece together the story of their aunt and uncle in Scotland and Canada; and to Rosalind (Pallot) Pett (daughter of Edward and Margaret Pallott) for confirming the details of her parents' wartime experience in Beauly.

Also, many thanks to the few remaining CFC men whom I was able to interview, and to their war brides, children, grandchildren, brothers, sisters, and in-laws who shared what they knew of the CFC story: Sewell Shaw of Woodstock (4 Company); the late Milford Kinney of Perth-Andover (4 Company); the late Alfred Blizzard, Jr., son of Alfred Blizzard, Sr. of Fredericton Junction (15 Company); George Campbell of Fredericton (25 Company); Jack Rutledge, nephew of Major Ralph S. Holmes of Doaktown (17 Company); Clair (Whelton) McCain, daughter of Bedford Whelton (15 Company); the late Joey Whelton, wife of Bedford Whelton; Betty Hudson, daughter of Hubert Gee (15 Company); Dolly Gunning, wife of Charlie Gunning (15 Company); Wendy Anderson, daughter of George Condley

(15 Company); Martha McCrae, sister of Duncan Campbell (15 Company); Karen Campbell, daughter-in-law of Duncan Campbell; the late Dr. Blair Orser, son of Arnold Orser (No. 5 District Headquarters, CFC); and Marie (O'Toole) Roy, daughter of Eddie O'Toole (15 Company). Thanks also to Kathleen Forsythe, daughter of Fred Cogswell (15 Company), for the photographs of her father during his service in the CFC.

In Beauly, many thanks to the MacIntosh brothers and sisters, Jeannie, Tommy, and Christine, whose childhood memories of 15 Company's camp at Lovat No. 2 brought a unique perspective on the Forestry Corps story. In Eskadale, thanks go to Mrs. Jessie Matheson, caretaker of St. Mary's, who kindly took me on a personal tour of the famed Lovat family church that played such an important part in my grandfather's Scottish experience.

Thank you to Val Sweeney, journalist with the *Inverness Courier*, whose articles on my research helped bring more stories of the CFC to my attention.

Thanks to Drusilla Fraser, wife of the late Hugh Fraser MP, who so graciously welcomed us to Balblair House in Beauly when we showed up unexpectedly on a sunny July day with a story about my grandfather's having been the cook there during the Second World War. And thanks to Joe Gibbs, owner of Phoineas House, the wartime headquarters of CFC operations in Scotland, who took time from a very busy day preparing for the annual Belladrum festival to show us a prized photograph of the Canadian officers who were stationed there during the war.

In Dingwall, thanks to Pauline Chapman, librarian, Dingwall School and Community Library, for her help in finding wartime newspaper articles about the Newfoundland Forestry Unit.

Thank you to Erica Munro-Ferguson of Novar House for taking us on a personal tour of her family home and allowing us to roam the estate and imagine what it must have been like when Wrens were billeted there.

Thank you to the staff of the Provincial Archives of New Brunswick in Fredericton, especially Allan Doiron, Twila Buttimer, Fred Farrell, and Johanna Aiton Kerr, for helping to preserve the hundreds of letters and archival documents that form the basis of this book and for always making it easy for me to access the documents whenever I asked.

To Ian Cameron of the Ballater Historic Forestry Project in Ballater, Scotland, thanks for your help in understanding the Newfoundland Forestry Unit's role in the Highlands during the war. And to Stuart Anderson, also of Ballater, thank you for sharing your own research and taking us on a whirlwind tour of what remains of the CFC in the area, including the camp at Dalmogie, where seven acres of sawdust are all that is left to remind us of the Forestry Corps.

Thank you genealogist Norrie Rudland of Edinburgh, who never said no when I asked for his help tracing the descendants of some of the people in this book. His indefatigable persistence paid off in finding more than one person whose stories we were able to flesh out thanks to his hard work, including John and Annie Mackie and Cecilia (Haggerty) Bird. To Charlene Skeels and her father Les Skeels, thank you for sharing the story of your grandmother and great-grandmother, Cecilia, bringing to a close a search that began in Manchester during the war.

Thanks to Dr. Bill Parenteau, who helped me sort out the details of life in the logging camps of 1930s New Brunswick, and to Dr. Tony Tremblay for the kind use of his work on Fred Cogswell, the poet of 15 Company.

Thank you to John Boers of the Association of Liberation Children. John's assistance in obtaining information about long-deceased veterans and their families helped me to connect with so many families, including those of Rosalind Pallot and Denise Laviolette.

Thank you to Bob Briggs for his assistance in sorting out the details of 15 Company and for making his extensive research on the CFC freely available online at freepages.genealogy.rootsweb.ancestry.com/~jmitchell/cfc.html.

Thank you to Library and Archives Canada for allowing me—sometimes on very short notice—to review audio and video files related to the CFC while I was in Ottawa.

Thanks to Anna Sander, archivist and curator of manuscripts at Balliol College, Oxford, who helped me with the history of the Oxford University courses given during the war. It's a small world: Anna's grandmother grew up in Fredericton Junction and Waweig!

Thank you to John Boileau of Halifax, who shed light on the monument to the CFC in Beauly.

Thanks to Dr. Mairie Stuart, University of the Highlands and Islands in Dornoch, Scotland, for sharing her interest in the Forestry Corps and the story of Alleyne Hubbard, whose experience joining the Newfoundland Forestry Unit and then the CFC, only to be killed in action in Nijmegen in November 1944, is becoming part of Scotland's war history as well.

To Ian Tester at FindMyPast.co.uk and the British Newspaper Archive, thank you for your generosity in giving me full access to these websites so that I could continue with my research. Through these online sources I was able to tell the full story behind many of the incidents that occurred in Scotland during my grandfather's stay there.

Thank you to Kay Brookland of Fredericton for helping to decipher and transcribe the hundreds of archival documents and nearly three thousand pages of war diaries that would have taken me months to untangle, and to Dorothy Loose, who volunteered to transcribe my grandfather's letters so that I could upload them to my website, LettersFromBeauly.com, and share them with the world. Thanks also to Katie Noonan for help with researching newspaper articles from the war years.

Thanks to Susan and Clayton Doige for taking me around London to the places my grandfather spoke of in his letters and for letting me revel in the moment under Marble Arch, where he walked in 1941.

Thank you to Zoe (Blair) Boone, my friend and fellow traveller, who has walked with me on this journey from Canada to Scotland three times since 2007, who enjoyed every moment as much as I did, and who had her own connection to the CFC story as a young Wren serving at Novar House during the Second World War. To her granddaughter Jennifer (Boone) Little, who helped reunite Rosie and Alfred after nearly seventy years, thank you!

Thanks to Rod O'Connell for his help finding photographs of Robert K. Allen at the Nepisiguit Centennial Musuem and Archives in Bathurst.

Thanks to summer students Lindsay White, Jessica McLaughlin, Rebecca Lavigne, Alexandra Erb, and Myriam Arsenault for scanning the thousands of letters and photographs that just kept coming out of the woodwork at the Doucet Hennessy House in Bathurst.

Thank you to the Elders of the Bathurst mission of the Church of Jesus Christ of Latter-day Saints for their help in scanning the original archival documents.

Last but not least, a huge thank you to my mother Lucy (Hennessy) Jarratt, who became my sounding board and source of vital information, since she is one of the few remaining witnesses to the events described in this book. Also my uncle, the late Dr. Robert Hennessy, who shared his memories of growing up on the farm and the war years; my late aunt, Anna (Hennessy) Wesenberg, and her daughter Halldis, who inherited the family penchant for saving things; to my sisters Sally and Theresa for giving me the bits and pieces of the Beauly story that had come their way over the years; and my cousin Dr. Colleen Hennessy, who shared whatever she could in telling this family story. Finally, to my husband Dan Weston, who deserves a medal for his patience and support these past seven years as I researched, wrote, and travelled far and wide documenting a story he knew was so important to me and to New Brunswick's military heritage.

Selected Bibliography

Manuscript Sources

Généalogie Nepisiguit Genealogy & Archives, Bathurst, New Brunswick.

Library and Archives Canada, RG24 16417-18, No. 5 District, Canadian Forestry Corps, War Diaries 1940-1945.

Library and Archives Canada, RG24 16437, 15 COY, Canadian Forestry Corps, War Diaries, 1940-1945.

Library and Archives Canada, Military Personnel Records.

Nepisiguit Centennial Museum and Cultural Centre. Bathurst, New Brunswick, Robert K. Allen Collection.

Nova Scotia Archives, Historical Vital Statistics.

Provincial Archives of New Brunswick, Hennessy Moran Fonds.

Newspapers

Aberdeen Press and Journal
Bathurst *Northern Light*
Fredericton *Daily Gleaner*
Globe and Mail
Inverness Courier
Montreal Gazette
New York Times
North Shore Leader
Saint John *Telegraph Journal*
Star Weekly
Vancouver Sun
Yorkshire Post

Websites

ARCH, Archaeology for Communities of the Highlands. Available at www.archhighland.org.uk.

Balliol College Archives & Manuscripts. Available at archives.balliol.ox.ac.uk.

Beauly, Black Isle and Muir of Ord Info. Available at black-isle.info.

Beautiful Beauly. Available at http://visitbeauly.com/history.php.

Bob Briggs Canadian Forestry Corps Website. Available at freepages.genealogy.rootsweb.ancestry.com/~jmitchell/cfc.html.

BBC. Available at news.bbc.co.uk.

British Newspaper Archive. Available at britishnewspaperarchive.co.uk.

Canadian Film and Photo Unit. Available at canadianfilmandphotounit.ca.

Canadian Virtual War Memorial. Available at veterans.gc.ca/eng/remembrance/memorials/canadian-virtual-war-memorial.

Canadian War Brides. Available at canadianwarbrides.com.

Clan Fraser. Available at clanfraser.org.

Find My Past. Available at findmypast.co.uk.

Historic Scotland. Available at historic-scotland.gov.uk.

In Memoriam. Available at inmemoriam.ca.

Letters from Beauly. Available at lettersfrombeauly.com.

K-Lines Internment Camp. Available at curragh.info.

Queen's University, Belfast. School of History and Anthropology. "Irish History Live: Northern Ireland and World War II." Available at qub.ac.uk.

St. Mary's Beauly. Available at stmarysbeauly.org.

78th Fraser Highlanders. Available at fortfrasergarrison.com.

U-Boat.net. Available at uboat.net.

Women's Timber Corps. Available at womenstimbercorps.com.

Other Sources

Bird, Will R. *North Shore (New Brunswick) Regiment*. Fredericton, NB: Brunswick Press, 1963.

Bowering, Clifford H. *Service: The Story of the Canadian Legion 1925-1960*. Montreal: Canadian Printing and Lithographic, 1960.

Canada. Department of National Defence. National Defence and the Canadian Forces. Historical Officer, Canadian Military Headquarters. "Canadian Forestry Corps 1941-1943." Report 97, June 1, 1943. Available online at cmp-cpm.forces.gc.ca/dhh-dhp/his/rep-rap/cmhqrd-drqgmc-eng.asp?txtType=2&RfId=101.

————. Department of National Defence. National Defence and the Canadian Forces. Historical Officer, Canadian Military Headquarters. "Canadian Forestry Corps 1943-1944." Report 117, May 25, 1944. Available online at cmp-cpm.forces.gc.ca/dhh-dhp/his/rep-rap/cmhqrd-drqgmc-eng.asp?txtType=2&RfId=117.

————. Department of National Defence. National Defence and the Canadian Forces. Historical Section, Canadian Military Headquarters. "The Canadian Forestry Corps 1944-1945." Report 151, March 18, 1946. Available online at cmp-cpm.forces.gc.ca/dhh-dhp/his/rep-rap/cmhqrd-drqgmc-eng.asp?txtType=2&RfId=151.

Canadian Army Film and Photo Unit. "Wood for War." Ottawa, 1941.

Cogswell, Fred. *A Long Apprenticeship: Collected Poems*. Fredericton, NB: Fiddlehead Poetry Books, 1980.

————. *When the Right Light Shines*. Ottawa: Borealis Press, 1992.

Curran, Tom. *They Also Served: The Newfoundland Overseas Forestry Unit 1939-1946*. St. John's: Jesperson's Press, 1987.

Forestry Chronicle 69, no. 2 (1993).

Halleday, Laurel. "'Ladies and Gentlemen, Soldiers and Artists': Canadian Military Entertainers 1939-1946." Master's thesis, University of Calgary, 2000.

Harper, Marjory. "Cossar's Colonists: Juvenile Migration to New Brunswick in the 1920s." *Acadiensis* 28, no. 1 (1998): 47-65.

Harrison, H.W. *The Village of Beauly: A Study of the History and Demography of the Village of Beauly 1700-2000*. Kilmorack, UK: Kilmorack Heritage Association, 2001.

Hickey, R.M. *The Scarlet Dawn*. Campbellton, NB: Tribune Publishers, 1949.

Jarratt, Melynda. *Captured Hearts: New Brunswick's War Brides*. Fredericton, NB: Goose Lane Editions, 2008.

————. *War Brides: The Stories of the Women Who Left Everything Behind to Follow the Men They Loved*. Stroud, UK: Tempus Publishing, 2007.

Klotz, Sarah. "Shooting the War: The Canadian Army Film Unit in the Second World

War." *Canadian Military History* 14, no. 3 (2005): 21-38. Available online at scholars.wlu.ca/cmh/vol14/iss3/3.

Kohli, Marjorie. *The Golden Bridge: Young Immigrants to Canada 1833-1939*. Toronto: Dundurn Press, 2003.

Kozar, Judy. *Canada's War Grooms and the Girls who Stole their Hearts*. Renfrew, ON: General Store Publishing House, 2007.

Kruse, Susan. *Boblainy Forest through the Ages*. With Ronald MacLean. Strathpeffer, UK: Archaeology for Communities of the Highlands, 2015.

————. "Evanton Wartime Remains." Strathpeffer, UK: Archaeology for Communities of the Highlands, September 30, 2013.

Lovat, Lord. *March Past: A Memoir by Lord Lovat*, 2nd ed. London: Weidenfield and Nicolson, 1979.

MacKay, Donald. *The Lumberjacks*. Toronto: McGraw-Hill Ryerson, 1978.

Maclean, Veronica. *Past Forgetting: A Memoir of Heroes, Adventure, Love and Life with Fitzroy Maclean*. London: Headline Book Publishing, 2003.

McCrae, Kenneth. *Highland Doorstep*. Edinburgh: Moray Press, 1953.

Miller, James. *The Foresters: The Story of Scotland's Forests*. Edinburgh: Birlinn, 2009.

Parenteau, Bill. "Forest and Society in New Brunswick: The Political Economy of the Forest Industries, 1918-1939." PhD diss., University of New Brunswick, 1994.

Parker, Gerry. *Workin' in the Woods: Toil for Timber in Early New Brunswick*. Sackville, NB: Gerry Parker, 2015.

Paterson, Anne-Mary. "Kilmorack: History of a Highland Parish." [n.p.]: Anne-Mary Paterson, 2012.

Soucoup, Dan. *Logging in New Brunswick: Lumber, Mills & River Drives*. Halifax, NS: Nimbus Publishing, 2011.

Stacey, C.P. *Official History of the Canadian Army in World War II*, vol. 1, *Six Years of War*. Ottawa: Queen's Printer, 1955.

Stanley, George. "The Canadian Forestry Corps 1940-1943." *Canadian Geographical Journal* 28, no. 3 (1944): 136-7.

Stewart, Mairie. *"The forest is a beautiful place to be": The Story of Forestry in The Great Glen in the 20th Century*. Touch Wood Oral History Project. Edinburgh: Forestry Commission Scotland, 2008.

————. *"No rivalry but different": Glenmore and Rothiemurchus in the 20th Century.* Touch Wood Oral History Project. Edinburgh: Forestry Commission Scotland, 2010.

————. *"Smell of the rosin, noise of the saw": The Story of Forestry in Mid-Argyll in the 20th Century.* Touch Wood Oral History Project. Edinburgh: Forestry Commission Scotland, 2007.

Thompson, Susan J., and H.W. Harrison. *A History of the Parish of Kiltarlity, Cill Taraghlain, Braigh na h'airde: A Monograph in Three Volumes on the Topography, History and Demography of the Parish and Its Townships,* vol. 3, part 1, *Kiltarlity: The Eastern Townships: Lord Lovat's Estate.* Kilmorack, UK: Kilmorack Heritage Association, 2006-10.

Tremblay, Tony. *Fred Cogswell: The Many-Dimensioned Self.* Fredericton, NB: University of New Brunswick, Electronic Text Centre, 2012. Available online at issuu.com/unb-etc/docs/cogswell.

Wonders, William. *The "Sawdust Fusiliers": The Canadian Forestry Corps in the Scottish Highlands in World War Two.* Montreal: Canadian Pulp and Paper Association, 1991.

Index

The New Brunswick Military History Museum

The mission of the New Brunswick Military History Museum is to collect, preserve, research, and exhibit artifacts which illustrate the history and heritage of the military forces in New Brunswick and New Brunswickers at war, during peacetime, and on United Nations or North Atlantic Treaty Organization duty.

The New Brunswick Military History Museum is proud to partner with the Gregg Centre.

Highlighting 400 years of New Brunswick's history.

The New Brunswick Military Heritage Project

The New Brunswick Military Heritage Project, a non-profit organization devoted to public awareness of the remarkable military heritage of the province, is an initiative of the Brigadier Milton F. Gregg, VC, Centre for the Study of War and Society of the University of New Brunswick. The organization consists of museum professionals, teachers, university professors, graduate students, active and retired members of the Canadian Forces, and other historians. We welcome public involvement. People who have ideas for books or information for our database can contact us through our website: www.unb.ca/nbmhp.

One of the main activities of the New Brunswick Military Heritage Project is the publication of the New Brunswick Military Heritage Series with Goose Lane Editions. This series of books is under the direction of J. Brent Wilson, Director of the New Brunswick Military Heritage Project at the University of New Brunswick. Publication of the series is supported by a grant from the Canadian War Museum.

The New Brunswick Military History Series

Volume 1
Saint John Fortifications, 1630-1956,
Roger Sarty and Doug Knight

Volume 2
*Hope Restored: The American Revolution and the Founding
of New Brunswick,* Robert L. Dallison

Volume 3
The Siege of Fort Beauséjour, 1755, Chris M. Hand

Volume 4
*Riding into War: The Memoir of a Horse Transport Driver,
1916-1919,* James Robert Johnston

Volume 5
*The Road to Canada: The Grand Communications Route from Saint John
to Quebec,* W.E. (Gary) Campbell

Volume 6
*Trimming Yankee Sails: Pirates and Privateers
of New Brunswick,* Faye Kert

Volume 7
*War on the Home Front: The Farm Diaries
of Daniel MacMillan, 1914-1927,*
edited by Bill Parenteau and Stephen Dutcher

Volume 8

Turning Back the Fenians: New Brunswick's Last Colonial Campaign,
Robert L. Dallison

Volume 9

*D-Day to Carpiquet: The North Shore Regiment and the Liberation
of Europe*, Marc Milner

Volume 10

*Hurricane Pilot: The Wartime Letters
of Harry L. Gill, DFM, 1940-1943*,
edited by Brent Wilson with Barbara J. Gill

Volume 11

*The Bitter Harvest of War: New Brunswick and the Conscription Crisis
of 1917*, Andrew Theobald

Volume 12

Captured Hearts: New Brunswick's War Brides,
Melynda Jarratt

Volume 13

*Bamboo Cage: The P.O.W. Diary of Flight Lieutenant Robert Wyse,
1942-1943*, edited by Jonathan F. Vance

Volume 14

*Uncle Cy's War: The First World War Letters
of Major Cyrus F. Inches*, edited by Valerie Teed

Volume 15

Agnes Warner and the Nursing Sisters of the Great War,
Shawna M. Quinn

Volume 16

New Brunswick and the Navy: Four Hundred Years,
Marc Milner and Glenn Leonard